Student Instruction Manual

Records Management

9th Edition

Judith Read
Instructor & Department Chair
Computer Information Systems
Portland Community College
Portland, Oregon

SOUTH-WESTERN
CENGAGE Learning™

SOUTH-WESTERN
CENGAGE Learning™

Simulation, Records Management
Ninth Edition
Judith Read

Vice President of Editorial, Business:
  Jack W. Calhoun

Vice President/Editor-in-Chief: Karen Schmohe

Senior Acquisitions Editor: Jane Phelan

Senior Developmental Editor: Penny Shank

Consulting Editor: Dianne Rankin

Associate Marketing Manager: Laura Stopa

Associate Content Project Manager: Jana Lewis

Senior Media Editor: Michael Jackson

Editorial Assistant: Anne Kelly

Manufacturing Coordinator: Kevin Kluck

Production Service: S4Carlisle Publishing
  Services

Senior Art Director: Tippy McIntosh

Internal Designer: Lou Ann Thesing

Cover Designer: Lou Ann Thesing

Cover Image: Media Bakery

ISBN-13: 978-0-538-73142-3
ISBN-10: 0-538-73142-7

South-Western Cengage Learning
5191 Natorp Boulevard
Mason, OH 45040
USA

Cengage Learning products are represented in Canada by Nelson Education, Ltd.

For your course and learning solutions, visit **www.cengage.com/school**

Printed in the United States of America
4 5 14 13

TABLE OF CONTENTS

Using the Records Management Simulation 1

Alphabetic Indexing Rules 2

Rule 1:   Indexing Order of Units 2
          A. Personal Names 2
          B. Business Names 2
Rule 2:   Minor Words and Symbols in Business Names 2
Rule 3:   Punctuation and Possessives 2
Rule 4:   Single Letters and Abbreviations 3
          A. Personal Names 3
          B. Business Names 3
Rule 5:   Titles and Suffixes 3
          A. Personal Names 3
          B. Business Names 3
Rule 6:   Prefixes—Articles and Particles 3
Rule 7:   Numbers in Business Names 4
Rule 8:   Organizations and Institutions 4
Rule 9:   Identical Names 4
Rule 10: Government Names 5
          A. Local and Regional Government Names 5
          B. State Government Names 6
          C. Federal Government Names 6
          D. Foreign Government Names 6

Cross-Referencing 7

Personal Names 7
          1. Unusual (Easily Confused) Names 7
          2. Hyphenated Surnames 8
          3. Alternate Names 8
          4. Similar Names 9
Business Names 10
          1. Compound Names 10
          2. Abbreviations and Acronyms 10
          3. Popular and Coined Names 11
          4. Hyphenated Names 11

5. Divisions and Subsidiaries   11
6. Changed Names   12
7. Similar Names   12
8. Foreign Business Names   13
9. Foreign Government Names   13

Subjects Within an Alphabetic Arrangement   14

Overview of Auric Systems, Inc.   15

Overview of Jobs 1–4   16

Directions for Jobs 1–4   17

Job 1   Alphabetic Filing Rules 1–4   17
Job 2   Alphabetic Filing Rules 5–8   21
Job 3   Alphabetic Filing Rules 9–10   23
Job 4   Alphabetic Filing Rules 1–10   25

Overview of Jobs 5–13   27

Directions for Jobs 5–13   30

Job 5   Correspondence Filing—Rules 1–5   30
Job 6   Correspondence Filing—Rules 6–10   37
Job 7   Correspondence Filing—Rules 1–10 and Tickler File Usage   41
Job 8   Requisition and Charge-Out Procedures   47
Job 9   Transfer Procedures   52
Job 10   Subject Correspondence Filing   56
Job 11   Consecutive Numeric Correspondence Filing   61
Job 12   Terminal-Digit Numeric Correspondence Filing   68
Job 13   Geographic Filing   74

USING THE RECORDS MANAGEMENT SIMULATION

This Student Instruction Manual consists of explanations and instructions for completing each of the 13 jobs in RECORDS MANAGEMENT SIMULATION, Ninth Edition. All the supplies necessary for completing the simulation are included in the simulation envelope. They are:

- Student Instruction Manual
- File Box
- Forms Pads 1 through 4
- Supplies Envelopes 1 and 2
- Data CD

Each job is performed in a simulated business environment and should be completed as directed by your instructor. You will proceed from the simple to the complex as you apply the alphabetic filing rules first to the cards and then, beginning with Job 5, to correspondence pieces. Methods of checking your completed work will vary. Check your work carefully as you complete each job before going on to the next job.

The most important filing concept to remember is that all filing is done to facilitate retrieving information when it is needed. To retrieve information efficiently, a set of rules must be followed. ARMA International has published *Establishing Alphabetic, Numeric and Subject Filing Systems,*[1] containing standard rules for storing records alphabetically. By using ARMA International's alphabetic indexing rules, businesses have a place to start setting up an efficient alphabetic storage system.

The rules presented in the RECORDS MANAGEMENT textbook and summarized here are written to agree with the standard filing rules presented in *Establishing Alphabetic, Numeric and Subject Filing Systems* published by ARMA International. It is extremely important that you learn these rules thoroughly. Referring to these rules is always permissible. A summary of the cross-referencing principles to be used with these jobs is also provided on the following pages of this Manual.

---

[1]ARMA International, *Establishing Alphabetic, Numeric and Subject Filing Systems* (Lenexa, KS: ARMA International, 2005), pp. 17–22.

ALPHABETIC INDEXING RULES

RULE 1: Indexing Order of Units

A. Personal Names

A personal name is indexed in this manner: (1) the surname (last name) is the key unit, (2) the given name (first name) or initial is the second unit, and (3) the middle name or initial is the third unit. If determining the surname is difficult, consider the last name written as the surname. (You will learn how to handle titles that appear with names in a later rule.)

A unit consisting of just an initial precedes a unit that consists of a complete name beginning with the same letter—*nothing before something*. Punctuation is omitted. Remember, the underscored letter in the examples in the textbook shows the correct order.

B. Business Names

Business names are indexed *as written* using letterheads or trademarks as guides. Each word in a business name is a separate unit. Business names containing personal names are indexed as written.

RULE 2: Minor Words and Symbols in Business Names

Articles, prepositions, conjunctions, and symbols are considered separate indexing units. Symbols are considered as spelled in full. When the word *The* appears as the first word of a business name, it is considered the last indexing unit.

Articles:	a, an, the
Prepositions:	at, in, out, on, off, by, to, with, for, of, over
Conjunctions:	and, but, or, nor
Symbols:	&, ¢, $, #, % (and, cent *or* cents, dollar *or* dollars, number *or* pound, percent)

RULE 3: Punctuation and Possessives

All punctuation is disregarded when indexing personal and business names. Commas, periods, hyphens, apostrophes, dashes, exclamation points, question marks, quotation marks, underscores, and diagonals (/) are disregarded, and names are indexed as written.

RULE 4: Single Letters and Abbreviations

A. Personal Names

Initials in personal names are considered separate indexing units. Abbreviations of personal names (Wm., Jos., Thos.) and nicknames (Liz, Bill) are indexed as they are written.

B. Business Names

Single letters in business and organization names are indexed as written. If single letters are separated by spaces, index each letter as a separate unit. An acronym (a word formed from the first, or first few, letters of several words, such as NASDAQ and ARCO) is indexed as one unit regardless of punctuation or spacing. Abbreviated words (Mfg., Corp., Inc.) and names (IBM, GE) are indexed as one unit regardless of punctuation or spacing. Radio and television station call letters (KDKA, WNBC) are indexed as one unit.

RULE 5: Titles and Suffixes

A. Personal Names

A title before a name (Dr., Miss, Mr., Mrs., Ms., Professor, Sir, Sister), a seniority suffix (II, III, Jr., Sr.), or a professional suffix (CRM, DDS, Mayor, M.D., Ph.D., Senator) after a name is the last indexing unit. Numeric suffixes (II, III) are filed before alphabetic suffixes (Jr., Mayor, Senator, Sr.). If a name contains a title and a suffix (Ms. Lucy Wheeler, DVM), the title *Ms* is the last unit.

Royal and religious titles followed by either a given name or a surname only (Princess Anne, Father Leo) are indexed and filed as written.

B. Business Names

Titles in business names (Capt. Hook's Bait Shop) are indexed as written. The word *The* is considered the last indexing unit when it appears as the first word of a business name.

RULE 6: Prefixes–Articles and Particles

A foreign article or particle in a personal or business name is combined with the part of the name following it to form a single indexing unit. The indexing order is not affected by a space between a prefix and the rest of the name (Alexander La Guardia), and the space is disregarded when indexing.

Examples of articles and particles are: a la, D', Da, De, Del, De La, Della, Den, Des, Di, Dos, Du, E', El, Fitz, Il, L', La, Las, Le, Les, Lo, Los, M', Mac, Mc, O', Per, Saint, San, Santa, Santo, St., Ste., Te, Ten, Ter, Van, Van de, Van der, Von, Von der.

RULE 7: Numbers in Business Names

Numbers spelled out (Seven Lakes Nursery) in business names are filed alphabetically. Numbers written in digits are filed before alphabetic letters or words (B4 Photographers comes before Beleau Building and Loan).

Names with numbers written in digits in the first units are filed in ascending order (lowest to highest number) before alphabetic names (229 Club, 534 Shop, First National Bank of Chicago). Arabic numerals are filed before Roman numerals (2 Brothers Deli, 5 Cities Transit, XII Knights Inn).

Names with inclusive numbers (20–39 Singles Club) are arranged by the first digit(s) only (20). Names with numbers appearing in other than the first position (Pier 36 Cafe) are filed alphabetically and immediately before a similar name without a number (Pier 36 Cafe comes before Pier and Port Cafe).

When indexing names with numbers written in digit form that contain *st, d,* and *th* (1st Mortgage Co., 2d Avenue Cinemas, 3d Street Pest Control), ignore the letter endings and consider only the digits (1, 2, 3).

When indexing names with a number (in figures or words) linked by a hyphen to a letter or word (A-1 Laundry, Fifty-Eight Auto Body, 10-Minute Photo), ignore the hyphen and treat it as a single unit (10Minute, A1, FiftyEight).

When indexing names with a number plus a symbol (55+ Social Center), treat it as a single unit (55plus).

RULE 8: Organizations and Institutions

Banks and other financial institutions, clubs, colleges, hospitals, hotels, lodges, magazines, motels, museums, newspapers, religious institutions, schools, unions, universities, and other organizations and institutions are indexed and filed according to the names written on their letterheads.

RULE 9: Identical Names

In correspondence files, determining which person or business is the correct one when there are others with identical names can be a challenge. When personal names and names of businesses, institutions, and organizations are identical (including titles, as explained in Rule 5), filing order is determined by the addresses. Compare addresses in the following order:

1. City names.

2. State or province names (if city names are identical).

3. Street names, which include *Avenue, Boulevard, Drive, Street,* (if city and state names are identical).

   a. When the first units of street names are written in digits (18th Street), the names are considered in ascending numeric order (1, 2, 3) and placed together before alphabetic street names (18th Street, 24th Avenue, Academy Circle).

b. Street names written as digits are filed before street names written as words (22nd Street, 34th Avenue, First Street, Second Avenue).

c. Street names with compass directions (North, South, East, and West) are considered as written (SE Park Avenue, South Park Avenue).

d. Street names with numbers written as digits after compass directions are considered before alphabetic names (East 8th Street, East Main Street, Sandusky Drive, SE Eighth Avenue, Southeast Eighth Street).

4. House or building numbers (if city, state, and street names are identical).

a. House and building numbers written as digits are considered in ascending numeric order (8 Riverside Terrace, 912 Riverside Terrace) and placed together before spelled-out building names (The Riverside Terrace).

b. House and building numbers written as words are filed after house and building numbers written as digits (11 Park Avenue South, One Park Avenue).

c. If a street address and a building name are included in an address, disregard the building name.

d. ZIP Codes are not considered in determining filing order.

RULE 10: Government Names

Government names are indexed first by the name of the governmental unit—city, county, state, or country. Next, index the distinctive name of the department, bureau, office, or board.

A. Local and Regional Government Names

The first indexing unit is the name of the county, parish, city, town, township, or village. *Charlotte Sanitation Department* is an example. *Charlotte* (a city) would be the first indexing unit. Next, index the most distinctive name of the department, board, bureau, office, or government/political division. In this case, *Sanitation* would be the most distinctive name of the department. The words *County of, City of, Department of,* etc., are added for clarity and are considered separate indexing units. If *of* is not a part of the official name as written, it is not added as an indexing unit. Five examples follow.

Filing Segment		Indexing Order of Units			
Name	Key Unit	Unit 2	Unit 3	Unit 4	Unit 5
1. County of Alameda Aquatic Center	Alameda	County	of	Aquatic	Center
2. City of Arlington Public Library	Arlington	City	of	Public	Library
3. City of Arlington Senior Center	Arlington	City	of	Senior	Center
4. Ashley County Department of Elections	Ashley	County	Elections	Department	of
5. Augusta City Water Works	Augusta	City	Water	Works	

B. State Government Names

Similar to local and regional political/governmental agencies, the first indexing unit is the name of the state or province. Then index the most distinctive name of the department, board, bureau, office, or government/political division. The words *State of, Province of, Department of,* etc., are added for clarity and are considered separate indexing units. If *of* is not a part of the official name as written, it is not added as an indexing unit. Two examples follow.

Filing Segment	Indexing Order of Units				
Name	**Key Unit**	**Unit 2**	**Unit 3**	**Unit 4**	**Unit 5**
1. Michigan Department of Education	Michigan	Education	Department	of	
2. Michigan State Police	Michigan	State	Police		

C. Federal Government Names

Use three indexing "levels" (rather than units) for the United States federal government. Consider *United States Government* as the first level. The second level is the name of a department or top-level agency that is rearranged to show the most distinctive part first; for example, *Agriculture Department (of)*. Level three is the next most distinctive name; for example, *Forest Service*. The words *of* and *of the* are extraneous and should <u>not</u> be considered when indexing. These words are shown in parentheses for reference only. Two examples follow.

Filing Segment		
	Level 1 United States Government	
Name	**Level 2**	**Level 3**
1. National Weather Service, Department of Commerce	Commerce Department (of)	National Weather Service
2. Office of Civil Rights, Department of Education	Education Department (of)	Civil Rights Office (of)

D. Foreign Government Names

The name of a foreign government and its agencies is often written in a foreign language. When indexing foreign names, begin by writing the English translation of the government name on the document. The English name is the first indexing unit. Then index the balance of the formal name of the government, if needed, or if it is in the official name (China Republic of). Branches, departments, and divisions follow in order by their distinctive names. States, colonies, provinces, cities, and other divisions of foreign governments are followed by their distinctive or official names as spelled in English.

CROSS-REFERENCING

Some records of persons and businesses may be requested by a name that is different from the one by which it was stored. This is particularly true if the key unit is difficult to determine. When a record is likely to be requested by more than one name, an aid called a cross-reference is prepared. A **cross-reference** shows the name in a form other than that used on the original record, and it indicates the storage location of the original record. The filer can then find requested records regardless of the name used in the request for those records. A copy of the document may be stored in the cross-reference location or a cross-reference sheet may be prepared.

Four types of personal names should be cross-referenced:

1. Unusual (easily confused) names
2. Hyphenated surnames
3. Alternate names
4. Similar names

Nine types of business names should be cross-referenced:

1. Compound names
2. Names with abbreviations and acronyms
3. Popular and coined names
4. Hyphenated names
5. Divisions and subsidiaries
6. Changed names
7. Similar names
8. Foreign business names
9. Foreign government names

Personal Names

Cross-references should be prepared for the following types of personal names.

1. Unusual (Easily Confused) Names

When determining the surname is difficult, use the last name written as the key unit on the original record. Prepare a cross-reference with the first name written as the key unit. An example is *Charles David.* On the original correspondence for Charles David, *David* is the key unit, and *Charles* is the second unit. The cross-reference sheet would show *Charles* as the key unit and *David* as the second unit. Someone looking under *Charles* would find the cross-reference that shows the original record is filed under D for David. Two additional examples follow.

Coded Filing Segment	Cross-Reference
2 Charles / David	2 Charles / David SEE David Charles
2 Gee-Hong / Cheung	2 GeeHong / Cheung SEE Cheung GeeHong
2 Keooudon / Sayasene	2 Keooudon / Sayasene SEE Sayasene Keooudon

2. Hyphenated Surnames

Hyphenated surnames often are used by married women. With hyphenated surnames, a request for records could be in either of the two surnames. A cross-reference enables retrieval in either case. An example is *Wendy Reardon-Bruss* shown below.

Many men use hyphenated surnames that are their family names, and they are known only by their hyphenated surnames. A cross-reference is not necessary. If men choose to adopt a hyphenated surname when they marry and may, in that case, be known by more than one name, a cross-reference is needed. See *Douglas Edwards-Read* shown below. You will be told when a cross-reference is needed for a man's name; otherwise, a cross-reference will not be required.

Coded Filing Segment	Cross-Reference
2 Wendy / Reardon-Bruss	2 3 Bruss / Wendy / Reardon SEE ReardonBruss Wendy
2 Douglas / Edwards-Read	2 3 Read / Douglas / Edwards SEE EdwardsRead Douglas

3. Alternate Names

When a person is known by more than one name, a cross-reference is needed. Examples are *Michelle Starkinsky* doing business as *Michelle Star* and *Faith Moran,* who is also known by three other names.

Coded Filing Segment	Cross-Reference
2 Michelle / <u>Star</u>	2 <u>Starkinsky</u> / Michelle SEE Star Michelle
2 Faith / <u>Moran</u>	2 <u>MorganRipley</u> / Faith SEE Moran Faith
	--------------------------------
	2 3 <u>Ripley</u> / Michael / Mrs SEE Moran Faith
	--------------------------------
	2 3 <u>Ripley</u> / Faith / Mrs SEE Moran Faith

4. Similar Names

A variety of spellings exist for some names like *Brown* and *Johnson*. A SEE ALSO cross-reference is prepared for all likely spellings. A SEE ALSO sheet directs the filer to multiple locations for related information. If the name is not found under one spelling, the filer checks the SEE ALSO sheet for other possible spellings. Two examples follow.

Coded Filing Segment	Cross-Reference
<u>Brown</u> SEE ALSO Browne, Braun, Brawn	<u>Browne</u> SEE ALSO Brown, Braun, Brawn
	--------------------------------
	<u>Braun</u> SEE ALSO Brown, Brawn, Browne

	<u>Brawn</u> SEE ALSO Brown, Browne, Braun
<u>Johnson</u> SEE ALSO Johnsen, Johnston, Jonson	<u>Johnsen</u> SEE ALSO Johnson, Johnston, Jonson
	--------------------------------
	<u>Johnston</u> SEE ALSO Johnson, Jonson, Johnsen
	<u>Jonson</u> SEE ALSO Johnson, Johnsen, Johnston

Business Names

Cross-references should be prepared for the following types of business names. The original name is the name appearing on the letterhead.

1. Compound Names

When a business name includes two or more individual surnames, prepare a cross-reference for each surname other than the first. In the following example, two cross-references are needed for the name *Jarvis, Rasmussen, and Sheraden Antiques.*

Coded Filing Segment	Cross-Reference
2 3 4 5 Jarvis, / Rasmussen, / and / Sheraden / Antiques	2 3 4 5 Rasmussen / Sheraden / and / Jarvis / Antiques SEE Jarvis Rasmussen and Sheraden Antiques 2 3 4 5 Sheraden / Jarvis / and / Rasmussen / Antiques SEE Jarvis Rasmussen and Sheraden Antiques

2. Abbreviations and Acronyms

When a business is commonly known by an abbreviation or an acronym, a cross-reference is prepared for the full name. Two examples are *MADD* (Mothers Against Drunk Driving) and *EZ Electronics* (Ewen and Zucker Electronics).

Coded Filing Segment	Cross-Reference
MADD	2 3 4 Mothers / Against / Drunk / Driving SEE MADD
2 EZ / Electronics	2 3 4 Ewen / and / Zucker / Electronics SEE EZ Electronics 2 3 4 Zucker / and / Ewen / Electronics SEE EZ Electronics

3. Popular and Coined Names

Often a business is known by its popular or coined name. The official name is shown on the original record. To assist in retrieving, a cross-reference is prepared for the popular name. Two examples follow.

Coded Filing Segment	Cross-Reference
2 3 4 5 Fred / Meyer / One / Stop / Shopping	Freddys SEE Fred Meyer One Stop Shopping
2 3 Smiths / Homestyle / Eatery	Smittys SEE Smiths Homestyle Eatery

4. Hyphenated Names

Many business names include hyphenated surnames. Like hyphenated personal names, business surnames with hyphens need to be cross-referenced for each surname combination. Two examples follow.

Coded Filing Segment	Cross-Reference
2 3 Jolly-Reardon / Consulting / Co.	2 3 ReardonJolly / Consulting / Co SEE JollyReardon Consulting Co
2 3 Heckman-O'Connor / Tour / Guides	2 3 OConnorHeckman / Tour / Guides SEE HeckmanOConnor Tour Guides

5. Divisions and Subsidiaries

When one company is a subsidiary or a division or branch of another company, the name appearing on the letterhead of the branch or subsidiary is the one indexed on the original record. A cross-reference is made under the name of the parent company. Two examples follow.

Coded Filing Segment	Cross-Reference
2 3 Ricoh / Business / Systems (a division of Ricoh USA)	2 Ricoh / USA SEE Ricoh Business Systems
2 Micro-Weld / Operations (a subsidiary of Kintech Corporation)	2 Kintech / Corporation SEE MicroWeld Operations

6. Changed Names

A company may change its name. Records must then be changed to indicate the name change and to ensure that the new name will be used for storage purposes. If only a few records are already in storage, they are usually re-filed under the new name, and the former name is marked as a cross-reference. If many records are filed under the former name, a permanent cross-reference is placed at the beginning of the records for the former name. Any new records are placed under the new name. In the following examples, *AT&T Wireless* changed its name to *Cingular Wireless,* and *Hershey Foods Corporation* changed its name to *The Hershey Co.*

Coded Filing Segment	Cross-Reference
2 Cingular / Wireless	2 ATandT / Wireless SEE Cingular Wireless
3 2 The / Hershey / Co.	2 3 Hershey / Foods / Corporation SEE Hershey Co The

7. Similar Names

A SEE ALSO cross-reference is used to alert the filer to check other possible spellings for a business name. The complete business name is not cross-referenced—only the similar name. Similar names for a business include examples like *Northwest* or *North West, Southeast* or *South East, Goodwill* or *Good Will,* and *All State* or *Allstate.* If a name could be considered either as one unit or as two units, it is a good candidate for a cross-reference. Two examples follow.

Coded Filing Segment	Cross-Reference
2　　　3 Allstate / Insurance / Co.	2 All / State SEE ALSO Allstate
2　　3　　4 South / East / Distribution / Co.	Southeast SEE ALSO South East

8. Foreign Business Names

Write the English translation of the foreign business name on each document to be stored and store the document under the English spelling. Prepare a cross-reference sheet using the foreign spelling as written in the native language, using the first word as the key unit. Two examples follow.

Coded Filing Segment	Cross-Reference
2 Humboldt / University	Humboldt-Universität SEE Humboldt University
2 Venezuelan / Line	2　　　3 Venezolana / de / Navegacion SEE Venezuelan Line

9. Foreign Government Names

The name of a foreign government and its agencies, like foreign businesses, is often written in a foreign language. Write the English translation of the government name on each document to be stored. Store all documents under the English spelling. Prepare a cross-reference sheet using the foreign spelling as written in its native language, using the first word as the key unit. Two examples follow.

Coded Filing Segment	Cross-Reference
2　　　3　　4 Federal / Republic / of / Brazil	2　　　3　　4 República / Federativa / do / Brasil SEE Brazil Federal Republic of
2　　3 Kingdom / of / Bhutan	Druk-yul SEE Bhutan Kingdom of

SUBJECTS WITHIN AN ALPHABETIC ARRANGEMENT

Within an alphabetic arrangement, records may sometimes be stored and retrieved more conveniently by a subject title than by a specific name. Beware, however, of using so many subjects that the arrangement becomes primarily a subject arrangement with alphabetic names as subdivisions. A few typical examples of acceptable subjects to use within an otherwise alphabetic name arrangement are:

- **Applications.** The job for which individuals are applying is more important than are the names of the applicants.

- **Bids or projects.** All records pertaining to the same bid or the same project are kept together under the project or bid title.

- **Special promotions or celebrations.** All records relating to a specific event are grouped together by subject.

When coding a record, the main subject is the key unit. Subdivisions of the main subject are considered as successive units. The name of the correspondent (individual or company name) is considered last. For example, on all records pertaining to applications, the word *Applications* is written as the key unit. The specific job applied for is a subdivision of that main subject and is the next unit (*Assistant,* for example). The applicant's name is coded last.

Indexing Order of Units

Key Unit	Unit 2	Unit 3	Unit 4	Unit 5
1. Applications	Assistant	Bianchi	Jason	
2. Applications	Assistant	Fung	Brenda	
3. Applications	Cashier	Corbett	Lucy	
4. Applications	Cashier	Jennings	Kenneth	
5. Applications	Data	Entry	Neally	Joyce
6. Applications	Data	Entry	Rodrigez	Luis

OVERVIEW OF AURIC SYSTEMS, INC.

Congratulations! You have been hired as the records manager for Auric Systems, Inc., a company that sells 3G and 4G cell phones and broadband internet access to individuals, companies, and government agencies. As you can see from the organization chart below, you work in the Chicago office and report to the president of the company, Terri Williams. There are two vice presidents: Glen Norris, who is in charge of the Customer Service Division, and Pat Johnson, who is in charge of the Broadband Communications Division. Auric Systems, Inc. uses a combination of paper and computerized records.

Auric Systems, Inc.

1100 W. Tell Avenue, Chicago, IL 60657-1100 Phone: 312-555-0100 Fax: 312-555-0102

Organization Chart

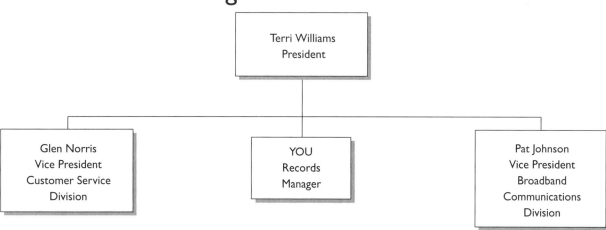

Your duties as records manager for Auric Systems, Inc. include filing in alphabetic order name cards for the cell phone customers. When completing the application activities in Chapters 1 through 4 of RECORDS MANAGEMENT, Ninth Edition, you used names only to practice alphabetic indexing rules 1–10. In the first four jobs of this simulation, you will apply the alphabetic indexing rules using cards bearing the names and addresses of cell phone customers.

Applying the alphabetic indexing rules to cards requires attention to detail and following correct procedures. The latter is accomplished with the aid of a set of uniform indexing rules. These rules are printed in the front of this Manual and further illustrated in the RECORDS MANAGEMENT text. You will gradually commit the rules to memory as you work with them.

All the supplies you need to complete each job are provided in the simulation envelope. Proceed according to the directions provided for each job. Instructions include a statement concerning the nature of the work to be done; a list of supplies to be used, directions for any assembling necessary; and step-by-step procedures to be followed. Giving careful attention to detail and systematically following the directions step by step will simplify your work.

Each job includes a computer activity. These activities demonstrate how databases and other electronic applications help with filing and records management. Your instructor will tell you if you should complete these activities.

After you have completed each job, check your work carefully. You will be instructed to fill out a Report Sheet and submit it to your instructor as directed. Report Sheets are provided as *Word* files on the Data CD. When you have completed an assignment requiring the alphabetic arrangement of a group of names, be prepared to explain the order of your arrangement.

Your instructor may direct you to take Finding Tests as you complete Jobs 1 through 4. Finding Test forms are provided as *Word* files on the Data CD.

IMPORTANT: Do not remove any guides or cards from your files unless the job instructions or your instructor directs you to do so. Save all database files and objects (tables, queries, and reports) you create while completing this simulation. These files may be used in a later job.

DIRECTIONS FOR JOBS 1–4

Job 1

Alphabetic Filing Rules 1–4

The principles and rules for indexing, coding, cross-referencing, and storing (filing) for Rules 1–4 are applied in this job. A customer information database is maintained for our cell phone users. Auric Systems, Inc. also maintains a correspondence file for paper documents. Your duties include filing in alphabetic order name cards for the cell phone customers.

Supplies Needed

- File box
- 5 one-fifth cut, first position, preprinted guides A, R, S, T, and U (Supplies 1 Envelope)
- 18 cards numbered 1 through 18 (Forms Pad 1)
- 7 blank cross-reference cards (Forms Pad 2)
- Report Sheet 1 (Data CD)
- Pencil

File Setup

1. In the packet of supplies, you will find a flat file box that must be unfolded to form a box. Press down on the labeled section to form a slot to hold your guides and cards. The ends of the box may be opened to allow you to store unused guides, folders, and records if you are interrupted before completing a job.

2. Remove five one-fifth cut, first position guides labeled A, R, S, T, and U from the Supplies 1 Envelope. In an office situation, guides for all letters of the alphabet would be present.

3. Place all guides in the file box in alphabetic order.

Filing Procedures

1. Carefully detach cards numbered 1 through 18 from Forms Pad 1. Keep the cards in proper numeric order as you detach them. Notice that cards are printed on the backs of Cards 1 through 18. Those cards will be used in future jobs.

2. Detach the seven cross-reference cards from Forms Pad 2, and place them in front of the A guide for use as they are needed. This is a convenient storage place for your unused cross-reference cards.

3. Separate the 18 cards into two groups—1 through 9 and 10 through 18. You will work first with cards numbered 1 through 9.

4. a. Code the name (shown in the first line of the address) on each printed card. Place a diagonal (/) between each unit, underline the key unit, and number the units after the key unit to show their sequence. Examples of the style to be used in coding names are as follows:

2 3 Karl / H. / <u>Harrison</u>	4 2 3 The / <u>Best</u> / Little / Bookstore
2 3 Laurie / D. / <u>Jacuzzi-Meister</u>	2 <u>By-the-Sea</u> / Motel
2 Ching-yu / <u>Kuo</u>	2 3 4 5 <u>U</u> / & / I / Day / Care

b. Mark a name that should be cross-referenced by placing an X beside the printed name on the original card.

c. Prepare the necessary cross-reference after you code the name requiring such a reference. In the upper right corner of the cross-reference card, write the number of the original card with an X after it. Code the cross-reference in the usual manner. (See the example below.) The first card requiring a cross-reference is Card 4 (Jennifer Taylor-Anderson).

> **CROSS-REFERENCE**
> 2   3   4X
> <u>Anderson</u> / Jennifer / Taylor
> SEE TaylorAnderson Jennifer

d. As you code Cards 1 through 9, you may find these comments helpful:

Card 1:   Name transposition is all that is required.

Card 2:   This is a business name; index it as written (Rule 1B).

Card 3:   Name transposition is all that is required.

Card 4:   Here is a hyphenated surname. Follow Rule 3 in coding, and prepare a cross-reference card. Write the number of the original card with an X after it on the cross-reference card. Code the cross-reference card as shown in the example above.

Card 5:   Prepare a cross-reference for this business acronym.

Card 6:   Here is another hyphenated surname. Prepare a cross-reference card.

Card 7:   Transposition is required.

Card 8:   Refer to Rule 1B, Rule 2, and Rule 4B.

Card 9:   Prepare a cross-reference for this unusual name.

5. After you have coded the names and prepared the necessary cross-references, sort the original and cross-reference cards into piles. Use one pile for each of the alphabetic guides A and R through U, according to the first letter of the key unit.

6. File the original and cross-reference cards in alphabetic order behind the appropriate guides in the file box.

7. Check your filing order carefully, shifting the position of any card that is misfiled.

8. Check your work by comparing your filing order with the filing order given here. Read from front to back behind the guides A, R, S, T, and U. Note that you will read the columns below from bottom to top.

1				
4X				
7	8			
2	6	5X		6X
9X	9	5	4	3
Front	**Front**	**Front**	**Front**	**Front**
A	**R**	**S**	**T**	**U**

9. Follow the directions given in Steps 4a through 4d for the remaining cards (numbers 10 through 18). Cross-references are needed for Cards 11, 13, and 14.

10. After you have coded the names and prepared the necessary cross-references for cards 10 through 18, sort the original and cross-reference cards into piles. Use one pile for each of the alphabetic guides A and R through U, according to the first letter of the key unit.

11. Interfile cards 10 through 18 with cards 1 through 9. Check your filing order carefully. Move any cards that have been misfiled.

12. Print the *Word* file *Report Sheet 1* found in the data files. In the A, R, S, T and U columns (corresponding to the guides in your file), list the numbers of the cards as they are filed in order behind each guide. Start the listing of numbers at the *bottom* of each column so that the numbers will appear in the same order from front to back as do the cards that are filed in the box. Also be sure to list cross-references with an X. Submit Report Sheet 1 as your instructor directs.

13. When your work has been checked, review any rules for alphabetic indexing that have caused you difficulty in this job. If necessary, change the order of the cards in your box so that they are filed correctly.

14. **IMPORTANT:** Do not remove the guides and cards from your file box.

15. If your instructor directs, take Finding Test 1. Print the *Word* file *Finding Test 1 Form* found on the Data CD. Locate each card as requested, and write your answers on the appropriate columns of the form.

Computer Activity

1. Locate the *Access* file *Job 1 Customers* in the data files. Copy the file to your working folder on a hard drive or removable storage device.

2. Open the Wireless table, which contains records for cell phone customers. The data for Cards 1 and 2 have been entered for you in the Wireless table. The ID field is a Number field; all other fields are text fields.

3. Enter the data from Cards 3 to 18 into the Wireless table. Key the card number in the ID field. Key the company or organization name in the Organization field. Do not enter the cross-reference information. You may wish to use an AutoForm to make entering the data easier.

4. Create a query to display a list of businesses and their phone numbers. Base the query on the Wireless table. Include the ID, Organization, and Phone fields in the results table.

5. Sort the records in ascending order by the Organization field. Enter an asterisk (*) in the Criteria row in the Organization field. This will cause only records with data in the field to appear in the query results.

6. Save the query as **Businesses Query.** Run the query and print the query results table.

7. How many records are in the query results table?

8. Which organization has ID number 16?

9. If you did a manual sort of these organizations for storing in an alphabetic filing system, which name would come first?

Important: Save all database files and objects (tables, queries, and reports) you create while completing this simulation. These files may be used in a later job.

Care of Supplies

Keep the guides and cards intact in your file drawer. You will add more items to the file drawer in Job 2.

Job 2

Alphabetic Filing Rules 5–8

The principles and rules for indexing, coding, cross-referencing, and filing for Rules 5–8 are applied in this job. You will file in alphabetic order additional customer name cards.

Supplies Needed

- File box with guides from Job 1
- The preprinted NUMBERS guide (Supplies 1 Envelope)
- 18 cards numbered 19 through 36 (Forms Pad 1)
- 6 blank cross-reference cards (Forms Pad 2)
- Report Sheet 2 (Data CD)
- Pencil

File Setup

1. Remove the NUMBERS guide from the Supplies 1 Envelope.

2. Place the NUMBERS guide in front of the file box. The guides should be in this order: NUMBERS, A, R, S, T, and U.

Filing Procedures

1. Carefully detach cards numbered 19 through 36 from Forms Pad 1. Keep the cards in numeric order as you detach them.

2. Detach six blank cross-reference cards from Forms Pad 2 and place them in front of the NUMBERS guide for use as they are needed.

3. a. Code the name on each card in the same manner as you coded the names in Job 1, referring to the alphabetic indexing rules as needed.

   b. Mark a name that should be cross-referenced by placing an X beside the printed name on the original card.

   c. Prepare the necessary cross-references on the blank cross-reference cards. If needed, refer to page 18 of this Manual for proper cross-reference card format.

   d. Code the cross-reference cards.

   e. As you code Cards 19 through 36, you may find these comments helpful:

   Card 19: This business changed its name.

   Card 20: This is a compound business name.

   Card 21: Refer to Rule 5 for personal titles and suffixes.

   Card 22: Prepare a similar name SEE ALSO cross-reference.

   Card 23: This customer has an alternate name. Prepare a cross-reference card for the alternate name.

   Card 24: Refer to Rule 6 for articles and particles.

Card 26:	This is a compound business name.
Card 29:	Refer to Rule 7 for business names that include numbers.
Card 31:	AB Associates is a division of Andrews, Inc.
Card 35:	Refer to Rule 6 for articles and particles.

4. Sort the original and cross-reference cards into piles. Use one pile for each of the six guides, according to the first letter or the number of the key unit.

5. Interfile the original and cross-reference cards in alphabetic or numeric order with the cards from Job 1.

6. Check the accuracy of the filing order; move any cards that have been misfiled.

7. Print the *Word* file *Report Sheet 2* found in the data files. List the numbers of the cards as they are filed in order behind each guide. You will list the cards from both Jobs 1 and 2. Start the listing of numbers at the *bottom* of each column so that the numbers will appear in the same order from front to back as do the cards that are filed in the box. List cross-reference cards with an X. Submit Report Sheet 2 as your instructor directs.

8. When your work has been checked, review any alphabetic indexing or cross-referencing rules that have caused you difficulty in this job. If necessary, change the order of the cards in your box so that they are filed correctly.

9. **IMPORTANT:** Do not remove the guides and cards from your file box.

10. If your instructor directs, take Finding Test 2. Print the *Word* file *Finding Test 2 Form* found in the data files. Locate each card as requested, and write your answers in the appropriate columns of the form.

Computer Activity

1. Locate the *Access* file *Job 1 Customers* that you updated in Job 1. Make a copy of the file and name it *Job 2 Customers.* Open the *Job 2 Customers* file.

2. Open the Wireless table. Enter the data from Cards 19 to 36 into the Wireless table. Key the card number in the ID field. Key the company or organization name in the Organization field.

3. Create a query to display a list of individuals (not businesses) who are located in cities other than Chicago. Base the query on the Wireless table. Include the ID, Title, First Name, Middle Name, Last Name, Suffix, and City fields in the results table.

4. Sort the records in ascending order by the ID field. Enter an asterisk (*) in the Criteria row in the Last Name field. Enter **Not "Chicago"** in the Criteria row in the City field.

5. Save the query as **City Query.** Run the query and print the query results table.

6. How many individuals in the database are located in cities other than Chicago?

Care of Supplies

Keep the guides and cards intact in your file box. You will add more items in Job 3.

Job 3

Alphabetic Filing Rules 9–10

The principles and rules for indexing, coding, cross-referencing, and filing for Rules 9 and 10 are applied in this job. You will file in alphabetic order additional customer name cards.

Supplies Needed

- File box with the guides from Jobs 1 and 2
- 18 cards numbered 37 through 54 (Forms Pad 1)
- 6 blank cross-reference cards (Forms Pad 2)
- Report Sheet 3 (Data CD)
- Pencil

File Setup

The guides and cards should be intact from Jobs 1 and 2.

Filing Procedures

1. Detach cards numbered 37 through 54 from Forms Pad 1. Keep the cards in numeric order as you detach them. Detach six blank cross-reference cards from Forms Pad 2.

2. a. Code the name on each card in the same manner as you coded the names in Jobs 1 and 2, referring to the alphabetic indexing rules as needed. **Exception:** Code federal government names according to levels rather than units.

   b. Mark a name that should be cross-referenced by placing an X beside the printed name on the original card; prepare and code the necessary cross-references on the blank cards.

   c. As you code Cards 37 through 54, you may find these comments helpful:

   Cards 37, 41, 47:   These are federal government names. Refer to Rule 10C.

   Cards 39, 49, 52:   These are city government names. Refer to Rule 10A.

   Cards 42, 46, 50:   Refer to Rule 9 Identical Names.

   Cards 51, 54:   Refer to Rule 10D Foreign Government Names.

   Card 45:   The original card is filed by the English translation. Prepare a cross-reference card for the foreign spelling.

   Card 53:   The new name is the filing segment for the original card. Prepare three cross-references for the former compound name.

3. Sort the original and cross-reference cards into piles. Use one pile for each of the six guides, according to the first letter or the number of the key unit.

4. Interfile the original and cross-reference cards in alphabetic or numeric order with the cards from Jobs 1 and 2. Check the accuracy of the filing order; move any cards that have been misfiled.

5. Print the *Word* file *Report Sheet 3* found in the data files. List the numbers of the cards as they are filed in order behind each guide. <u>You will list the cards from Jobs 1, 2, and 3.</u> Start the listing of numbers at the *bottom* of each column so that the numbers will appear in the same order from front to back as do the cards that are filed in the box. List cross-reference cards with an X. Submit Report Sheet 3 as your instructor directs.

6. When your work has been checked, change the order of the cards in your box (if necessary) so that the cards are filed correctly.

7. If your instructor directs, take Finding Test 3. Print the *Word* file *Finding Test 3 Form* found in the data files. Locate each card as requested, and write your answers in the appropriate columns of the form.

Computer Activity

1. Locate the *Access* file *Job 2 Customers* that you updated in Job 2. Make a copy of the file and name it *Job 3 Customers*. Open the *Job 3 Customers* file. Open the Wireless table.

2. Enter the data from Cards 37 to 54 into the Wireless table. Key the card number in the ID field. Do not enter the cross-reference information. For names of foreign embassies (Cards 51 and 54), enter the English translation. For foreign company names (Card 45), enter the name as written—not the translation. For government names, enter the complete name that may be shown on two lines. For example, for Card 37 enter **Department of Commerce Chicago Office** in the Organization field. For Card 53, enter the new name.

3. Create a query to display a list of organizations and individuals who are located in the 312 telephone area code. Base the query on the Wireless table. Include the Organization, First Name, Last Name, and Phone fields in the results table.

4. Sort the records in ascending order by the Organization field and then by the Last Name field. Enter **312*** in the Criteria row in the Phone field.

5. Save the query as **Phone List.** Run the query and print the query results table.

6. How many individuals are listed in the 312 telephone area code?

7. How many organizations are listed in the 312 telephone area code?

8. In what telephone area code is All About You located?

Care of Supplies

1. When instructed to do so, remove the six guides from the box and store them in the Supplies 2 Envelope.

2. Remove the cards from the box and put them in numeric order from 1 through 54. Discard the used cross-reference cards. Store the printed cards in the Supplies 2 Envelope. Keep the empty file box for use in Job 4.

Job 4

Alphabetic Filing Rules 1–10

This job provides a thorough review of alphabetic indexing Rules 1–10. You will be filing in alphabetic and numeric order customer name cards for the Broadband Communications Division of Auric Systems, Inc.

Supplies Needed

- File box with no cards or guides in it
- The preprinted NUMBERS and A guides (Supplies 2 Envelope)
- 5 new one-fifth cut, first position, preprinted guides B, C, D, E, and I (Supplies 1 Envelope)
- 54 cards numbered 55 through 108 (printed on the back of cards 1–54; Supplies 2 Envelope)
- 12 blank cross-reference cards (Forms Pad 2)
- Report Sheet 4 (Data CD)
- Pencil

File Setup

1. Remove the NUMBERS and A guides from the Supplies 2 Envelope; remove the five new one-fifth cut, first-position guides labeled B, C, D, E and I from the Supplies 1 Envelope.

2. Place the guides in alphabetic order in the file box with the NUMBERS guide in front.

Filing Procedures

1. Put cards numbered 55–108 in numeric order. Detach 12 blank cross-reference cards from Forms Pad 2 and place them in front of the NUMBERS guide for use as needed.

2. Code the name on each card, consulting the alphabetic indexing rules if needed. Prepare cross-references as needed. Some names may require more than one cross-reference card. Card 108 (Alpha & Omega Services, Inc.) does not require a cross-reference.

3. Sort the cards into piles. Use one pile for each of the guides.

4. File the original and cross-reference cards in alphabetic or numeric order behind the appropriate guides in the file box.

5. Check the accuracy of your arrangement.

6. When your work has been checked, review any alphabetic indexing or cross-referencing rules that have caused you difficulty in this job. If necessary, change the order of the cards in your box so that they are filed correctly.

7. Print the *Word* file *Report Sheet 4* found in the data files. List the contents of your file on the report sheet as you have done in preceding jobs.

8. If your instructor directs, take Finding Test 4.

Computer Activity

1. Locate the *Access* file *Job 3 Customers* that you updated in Job 3. Make a copy of the file and name it *Job 4 Customers.* Open the *Job 4 Customers* file.

2. Make a copy of the Wireless table. Name the new table **Broadband.** Open the Broadband table. Select and delete all records in the table.

3. Open the Broadband table in Design view. Change the Field Size property for the Phone field to 20. Save the table and switch to Datasheet view. Enter the data from Cards 55 to 108 into the Broadband table. Follow the same procedures used in Job 3 for entering data.

4. Create a report to display a list of broadband customers and their phone numbers. Base the report on the Broadband table. Include the Organization, First Name, Last Name, and Phone fields in the report.

5. Sort the records in ascending order by the Organization field, then by the Last Name field, and then by the First Name field.

6. Save the report as **Broadband Phone List** and print the report.

7. What is the telephone number for 1 Way Direct Sales?

8. In what telephone area code is De Luna Hotel located?

9. What is the first name of the person named Ames whose telephone number is 312-555-0162?

Care of Supplies

1. When instructed to do so, remove the guides from the file box and store them in the Supplies 2 Envelope.

2. Remove the cards from the box and put them in numeric order from 1 through 54. Discard the used cross-reference cards. Store the printed cards in the Supplies 2 Envelope.

3. Keep the empty file box for use in Job 5.

OVERVIEW OF JOBS 5–13

In Jobs 1 through 4, you reported directly to the president of the company and had no interaction with the Customer Service and Broadband Communications Divisions. Beginning with Job 5, you will interact with both divisions as you file correspondence to and from Auric Systems, Inc. *Incoming Correspondence* refers to correspondence addressed to the company. *Outgoing Correspondence* refers to correspondence sent from the company. Your objectives are to file these pieces of correspondence in correct order and then use them to learn about ticker files, requisition and charge-out procedures, and transfer procedures. You will also practice filing by the subject, consecutive numbering, terminal digit, and geographic methods.

Even though only a small part of the correspondence for Auric Systems, Inc. can be examined in this series of jobs, you will work with different methods of filing and will experience a variety of filing situations. Many items not included in these jobs may have preceded or followed the pieces of correspondence with which you will be working. Enough correspondence is given, however, to show continuity and to illustrate the filing problems that may arise.

As records manager for Auric Systems, Inc., you report to Terri Williams, president of the company. Auric Systems, Inc. has two divisions: Customer Service and Broadband Communications. Pat Johnson is the vice president in charge of Broadband Communications. Glen Norris is vice president in charge of Customer Service. An organization chart of Auric Systems, Inc. is shown on page 15.

All records are kept in a centrally located area. Your duties include knowing not only how and where the records originate, but also where they are to be filed, the length of time they are to be kept, and the method of final disposition. In any well-managed office, knowing what to do with old correspondence—whether to destroy, to transfer to inactive files, or to archive records—is important. Determining what to retain and what to destroy is also a part of your work, and you will be making these decisions as you complete Job 9.

The materials in the jobs are designed to teach you to file correspondence so that it can be found readily when requested. This requires attention to detail and following correct procedures. The latter is accomplished with the aid of the same alphabetic indexing rules you applied in Jobs 1 through 4. Although variations in these rules are used in some offices to fit specific situations, the rules are representative of those used most frequently in business. You will be able to adapt to rule variations in an actual office as you gain experience with the files in that office.

In a typical filing situation in a wholesale distribution business, you might be required to file dealer and customer correspondence, invoices, application letters, letters concerning professional organizations, budget reports, and various other records. You might also be required to file magazine and newspaper clippings, pamphlets, maps, and circulars. In this simulation, you will work with only a limited segment of the Auric Systems, Inc. file contents.

Incoming Correspondence

As you work with the correspondence in these jobs, you will code names or subjects by placing diagonals between the units, underlining the key unit, and numbering succeeding units. On incoming correspondence, the name to be coded appears in either the letterhead or the signature line; code it there. You will be given specific instructions about the placement of coded subjects and numbers to be written on the pieces of correspondence as you work with the jobs requiring such coding.

A date stamp appears on each incoming piece of correspondence that indicates when the correspondence was received. The date is not used for filing purposes, but it may be used for tickler file notation determination, which is discussed later.

Special notations, such as initials near the signature block, may appear on some correspondence signifying that the letter has been released for filing. A handwritten instruction to open an individual folder or a note written to bring the letter to someone's attention at a future date may also appear on the document. If only a date is written at the bottom of the letter, that date is a tickler file notation and may be disregarded until Job 7.

Outgoing Correspondence

The name to be coded on outgoing correspondence is usually found in the letter address. On forms, the name to be coded is the name of the person or business to whom the form is addressed.

Some correspondence requires an answer. A copy of the answer may be included in the records to be filed and will have *COPY* printed across it. The name in the closing lines or the initials in the reference block at the bottom left of the correspondence will show who is responsible for the answer. Knowing the sender's name and department name helps the filer in determining the subject of the correspondence.

Form Letters

Some of the correspondence you will file consists of inquiries from people who ask similar questions. For these inquiries, answers can be routine, pending further specific information. Such requests are answered with a form letter, a copy of which is rarely filed. Instead, an administrative assistant prepares a form letter and marks on the original piece of correspondence a code indicating which form letter was sent and the date on which it was mailed. This notation eliminates the need for a copy of the form letter and saves space in the files. To ensure that follow-up information is sent or received, a reminder or **tickler file** is sometimes used. If a notation regarding the letter is made in a tickler file, the original piece of correspondence is marked to indicate this information.

Form letter designations used in these jobs are as follows:

1. **FL-A** indicates that Form Letter A was sent to answer a letter requesting information about cell phones.

2. **FL-B** indicates that Form Letter B was sent to acknowledge correspondence concerning job applications.

3. **FL-C** indicates that Form Letter C was sent to answer an inquiry about obtaining cable and/or Internet service.

An example of the notations you will find at the bottom of some of the records is shown here:

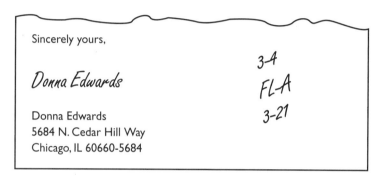

The notation near the signature block indicates that the letter was answered on March 4 with Form Letter A. The other date indicates that a reminder note for a tickler file (to be explained in Job 7) was made for March 21 so that this letter will be brought to the attention of the proper person on that date.

Release Marks

Records to be filed are released for storage in one of two ways: (1) by a notation near the signature block that a form letter has been sent on a specified date, or (2) by the initials of the president (TW) or one of the vice presidents (PJ or GN) near the signature block.

If a release mark is missing, place a check mark (✓) next to the piece number on the record, as well as on the report sheet. In an actual office, nothing is filed until it has been released. *Copies of letters (outgoing correspondence) and invoices do not need a release mark;* such records are considered ready for filing without that mark.

Job 5

Correspondence Filing—Rules 1–5

The objectives of this job are to inspect, index, code, cross-reference, sort, and file records alphabetically according to Rules 1–5.

Supplies Needed

- File drawer (box) with no cards or guides in it
- 7 one-fifth cut, first-position, preprinted guides (Supplies 2 Envelope) (used previously): NUMBERS, A, B, C, D, E, and I
- 1 one-fifth cut, second position, preprinted guide (Supplies 1 Envelope): APPLICATIONS
- 8 one-third cut, third position, preprinted folders (Supplies 1 Envelope): NUMBERS, A, B, C, D, E, I, and APPLICATIONS
- 1 one-third cut, third position, blank folder (Supplies 1 Envelope)
- 15 correspondence pieces numbered 1 through 15 (Forms Pad 2)
- 3 cross-reference sheets (Forms Pad 2)
- Sheet containing self-adhesive labels for Job 5 (Supplies 1 Envelope)
- Report Sheet 5 (Data CD)
- Pencil

Note: If you are interrupted before finishing any assignment, place all unfiled pieces and the drawer contents in the storage space at the bottom of the file drawer.

File Setup

1. Arrange the seven primary guides, the seven general alphabetic folders, and the special APPLICATIONS guide and folder so that the items in the file drawer are in the order shown in the illustration on page 31. Check to see that all general folders are the last items behind their correspondingly labeled guides. In a complete file, all of the letters of the alphabet would be included.

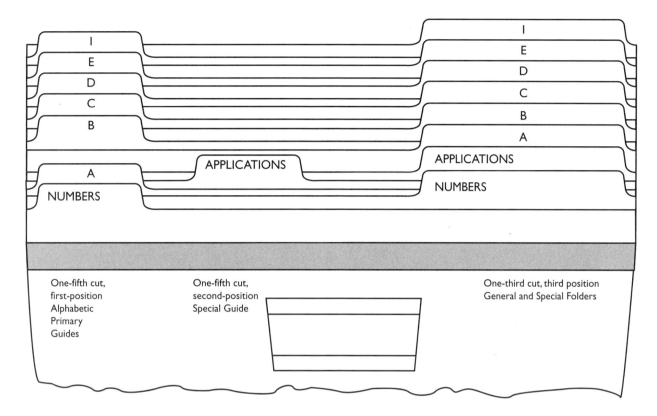

2.   Place the blank folder at the back of your file drawer for use as needed.

General Information

1.   Each piece of correspondence has its own number in the lower right corner. These numbers do not appear on correspondence in an actual business office; they are given here to help you easily identify the pieces in the jobs.

2.   The correspondence is dated from February through April.

3.   Examine and read each piece completely so that you can be sure it has been released for filing, you understand who wrote it, and you know the subject matter of the piece. This file is primarily a customer correspondence file, although other records are also included. Correspondence is filed by customer name with *two exceptions:* (1) All correspondence concerning applications for employment is filed in a separate section labeled APPLICATIONS. In a complete file, each position category would have a separate special folder labeled with the position being applied for. Because application correspondence is limited in this job, only one folder is necessary. Within that folder, all records are filed alphabetically by the name of the position applied for and then alphabetically by the applicant's name. The word *Applications* should be written on the correspondence and coded. (2) When customers order cable or Internet service, the invoice form is coded first by the word *Invoices* and then alphabetically by the customer name. The first invoice appears in Job 6.

4. A new individual folder is made if a special request that one be opened is written on any piece of correspondence. Also, after three or more pieces from, to, or about one correspondent have accumulated in a general folder, an individual folder is made for that correspondent. When a subject is added to the file, a special guide and folder must be made for that subject and filed in correct alphabetic order in the file. Because of the small number of pieces of correspondence in this simulation, you will find that several individual and special folders contain fewer than the usual three pieces, at the request of the president Terri Williams.

5. When a record is put into a folder, the top of the record is placed at the left. If there are two or more records for one correspondent, the most recently dated piece is placed at the front of the folder.

Filing Procedures

1. Carefully remove correspondence pieces numbered 1 through 15 from Forms Pad 2. You will work first with pieces 1 through 8.

2. Remove three cross-reference sheets from Forms Pad 2 and place them at the front of your file drawer for easy access while working.

3. Inspect each correspondence piece, 1 through 8, to see if it has been released for filing. A form letter notation is considered a release mark. Remember that a copy of an out-going letter (one written by Terri Williams, Glen Norris, or Pat Johnson) or an invoice is assumed to be ready for filing and, therefore, does not require a release mark. If the piece does not bear a release mark, place a check mark next to the piece number on the record. Disregard the tickler file notations at this time.

4. Mentally determine the name under which each piece is to be filed. Code each record according to previous coding instructions (place a diagonal between each unit, under-line the key unit, and number the other units). Refer to the following comments as you code pieces 1 through 8. You may refer to the indexing and cross-referencing rules at any time.

   #1: The letter has been released for filing since the notation shows that Form Letter A was sent on 3-4. When determining the name to be coded, do not be misled by the letterhead. A quick reading of the letter shows that Donna Edwards is requesting information for herself, not for the Holly Farm Inn. (She just used a piece of the hotel stationery on which to write.) Therefore, the letter should be coded under Donna Edwards' name. Place a diagonal between *Donna* and *Edwards,* underline the key unit of *Edwards,* and write a 2 over *Donna.* Keep your coded pieces in numeric order until you are told otherwise.

   #2: The release mark PJ appears on this letter. As indicated by the FAX cover note, Pat Johnson received this letter from The Crystal Net, Inc. by FAX. Code the filing segment in the letterhead: *Crystal* is the key unit, *Net* is the second unit, *Inc.* is the third unit, and *The* is the fourth unit.

#3:   Glen Norris has released this letter for filing. *Baker* is the underlined key unit, *Chas.* is unit 2, *S.* is unit 3, and *Mr.* is unit 4.

#4:   This letter, received by FAX, has been released by Glen Norris. The name to be coded appears in the letterhead. *Bekey* is the underlined key unit, *Almira* is unit 2, *R.* is unit 3, and *M.D.* is unit 4. A cross-reference is needed for the alternate name of *Mrs. Simon Carter.* Write an X in the margin opposite that name. Remove a blank cross-reference sheet from the file drawer. On the lines under Name or Subject, print *Carter Simon Mrs* and code the name. Write the date of the letter on the lines below Date of Record. Write a brief summary of the contents of the letter on the lines under Regarding. After SEE on the lines below Name or Subject, print the name by which the record is filed: *Bekey Almira R MD.* Write 5 after Job No. and 4X after Cross-Reference No.

CROSS-REFERENCE SHEET

Name or Subject

Carter/Simon/Mrs   (2 over Simon, 3 over Mrs)

_____

_____

Date of Record

March 5, 200–

_____

_____

Regarding

Changing Basic plan to Premium Programming package

_____

_____

_____

SEE

Name or Subject

Bekey Almira R MD

_____

Job No. ___5___   Cross-Reference No. ___4X___

#5:   The notation FL-B is the release mark. This letter discusses applying for a job. All application correspondence is filed in a separate subject folder. Write the word *Applications* at the top right of the letter and underline it. *Applications* is the key unit. The next units in the filing segment are the name of the position applied for: write *CSR* (for Customer Service Representative) after Applications. Place a diagonal between the two units, and code *CSR* with a 2. The next units are the applicant's name: place a diagonal between the two units and code *Carter* with a 3 and *Chris* with a 4.

#6:   The release mark GN appears on this letter. Note that it is written by Aleta Allison's secretary; however, do not code the secretary's name. Code the name that appears in the letterhead, Above & Beyond Insurance Co.

#7:   This letter has been released by Terri Williams. Code the business name in the letterhead.

#8:   The notation TW indicates that the letter has been released for filing. Code the business name in the letterhead.

5. After all eight pieces have been coded and the cross-reference sheet prepared, rough sort into six piles, matching the folder captions.

6. File the pieces in each pile in the proper folders. Check your work at this point as directed by your instructor.

7. Follow procedures 3 through 6 for correspondence pieces 9 through 15. Be sure to inspect each piece for a release mark. Comments about some of the pieces follow:

#9:   Prepare a cross-reference sheet for this unusual name of Allen R. David. A cross-reference will assist in retrieval if a request comes in for David R. Allen.

#10:   This business name is an acronym (ELITE, Inc.). Prepare a cross-reference sheet for the full name of the business.

#11:   This outgoing letter is in response to #6.

#13:   This outgoing letter, a FAX, is in response to #2.

#15:   This incoming letter is in response to #11.

Your instructor may give you further helpful information as you file pieces 9 through 15 with pieces 1 through 8.

8. Examine the contents of all the general folders to determine if three or more pieces of correspondence have accumulated for any one correspondent.

You will find that three pieces of correspondence for Above & Beyond Insurance Co. have accumulated in the A general folder. An individual folder should be prepared for this correspondent. Remove the blank folder from the back of your file drawer. Remove the sheet containing labels for Job 5 from the Supplies 1 Envelope. On the sheet you will find the label ABOVE AND BEYOND INSURANCE CO. In an office you would key the information on the label, but these labels have been prepared for your convenience. Attach the ABOVE AND BEYOND INSURANCE CO label on the tab of the blank folder. Remove the three pieces of correspondence to and from Above and

Beyond Insurance Co. from the A general folder and place them in correct date order (most recent one in front) in the new individual folder. File the individual folder in correct alphabetic order with the other folders in the file drawer.

9. Print the *Word* file *Report Sheet 5* found in the data files. List the contents of the folders, beginning with the folder at the front of the file drawer. Fill in Report Sheet 5 by starting at the *bottom* of each column. List cross-references with an X and unreleased pieces with a check mark. Keep your file drawer intact.

10. Check your report sheet as directed by your instructor.

11. If necessary, rearrange any items that were incorrectly filed and recode as needed. You will add items to your file drawer in Job 6. Job 5 does not have a Finding Test.

Computer Activity

Names and addresses for contacts who correspond with the company are recorded in an *Access* database. The records are used for creating labels and personalized correspondence as well as for answering questions about vendors, customers, and other correspondents. These records are stored in the Contacts table. Names and addresses for persons who apply for employment are stored in the Applicants table. In this activity, you will enter data in both tables.

1. Locate the *Access* file *Job 5 Contacts* in the data files. Copy the file to your working folder on a hard drive or removable storage device.

2. Enter the names and addresses from correspondence pieces 3 to 15 into the appropriate table. Records for pieces 1 and 2 have been entered for you as examples. When the correspondence relates to an application for employment, enter the data in the Applicants table. Enter records for all other correspondence in the Contacts table. Follow these guidelines when entering records:
   - Key the correspondence piece number in the ID field.
   - Read each piece of correspondence to determine data to enter in the Category field of the Contacts table:
     - When the correspondence relates to our company selling products or providing information that may lead to the sale of products, enter **Customer** in the Category field. Letters related to service requested or provided to current customers also go in the Customer category.
     - When the correspondence relates to our company buying products or requests or contains information that may lead to our company buying products, enter **Vendor** in the Category field. If the letter relates to a payment made by our company for any other reason, such as to pay taxes, enter **Vendor** in the Category field.
     - When the correspondence relates to other matters not mentioned above, enter **Other** in the Category field.
   - Records will not have information in all fields. For example, for correspondence from individuals, data will not be entered in the Company Name or Contact field.
   - The style for phone numbers varies on the correspondence. Use the style in the example records for all phone numbers. Some records will not have a phone number because no phone number is shown on the correspondence.

- Leave the country field blank for addresses in the United States. For other addresses, enter the state equivalent (province or region name) in the State field and the country in the Country field.
- Create only one record for each correspondent, even if there are two or more pieces of correspondence to or from the correspondent. You may wish to use an AutoForm to make entering the data easier.

3. Create a query to display a list of correspondents. Base the query on the Contacts table. Include the ID, Category, Company Name, First Name, and Last Name fields in the results table. Sort the records in ascending order by the Category field, the Company Name field, and the Last Name field.

4. Save the query as **Category Query.** Run the query and print the query results table.

5. In the Contacts table, how many records are for contacts outside the United States?

6. In what city is The Crystal Net, Inc. located?

7. How many records are in the Applicants table?

Care of Supplies

Keep the guides, folders, and correspondence pieces intact in your file drawer. You will add more items to the file drawer in Jobs 6 and 7. If labels for other jobs are on the same sheet as Job 5 labels, store the sheet of labels in the Supplies 1 Envelope for later use.

Job 6

Correspondence Filing—Rules 6–10

In this job your objective is to apply the principles and rules of filing records alphabetically according to Rules 6–10.

Supplies Needed

- File drawer with guides, folders, and correspondence pieces filed correctly as a result of Job 5
- 1 one-fifth cut, second position, preprinted guide (Supplies 1 Envelope): INVOICES
- 1 one-third cut, third position, preprinted folder (Supplies 1 Envelope): INVOICES
- 2 one-third cut, third position, blank folders (Supplies 1 Envelope)
- 15 correspondence pieces numbered 16 through 30 (Forms Pad 3)
- 5 cross-reference sheets (Forms Pad 2)
- Sheet of self-adhesive labels, Job 6 (Supplies 1 Envelope)
- Report Sheet 6 (Data CD)
- Pencil

File Setup

1. Place the INVOICES special guide and folder in proper order behind the I primary guide.

2. Place the blank folders at the back of your file drawer for use as needed.

Filing Procedures

1. Carefully remove correspondence pieces numbered 16 through 30 from Forms Pad 3.

2. Remove five cross-reference sheets from Forms Pad 2 and place them at the front of your file drawer for easy access while working.

3. Inspect each piece of correspondence to see if it has been released for filing. Remember to place a check mark next to the piece number on an unreleased record and on your report sheet. Outgoing correspondence and invoices do not need release marks. Disregard the tickler file notations at this time.

4. Mentally determine the name by which each record is to be filed. Code correspondence pieces 16 through 30. You may refer to the indexing and cross-referencing rules at any time. Comments about some of the pieces follow:

#16: This letter is from the Department of Tourism, Province of Alberta, Canada. The key unit is *Alberta.* The letter has been released for filing by TW; disregard the tickler file notation at this time.

#17: The English translation of this foreign business name is *International Computing Center.* Write the English translation at the top right of the letter and code the translation. A cross-reference should be prepared for the original spelling as shown in the illustration. Remember to write 17X at the bottom right of the cross-reference sheet. Follow the instructions on the letter to open an individual folder. Remove the printed label from the sheet of labels in the Supplies 1 Envelope. Keep the individual folder with your other coded pieces.

CROSS-REFERENCE SHEET

Name or Subject

        2   3   4

Centro / de / Computación / International

_____

_____

Date of Record

March 27, 200-

_____

_____

Regarding

Visit to Auric Systems, Inc., on April 14 at 9 a.m.

_____

_____

_____

SEE

Name or Subject

International Computing Center

_____

Job No. ___6___   Cross-Reference No. ___17X___

#18:   As you code this letter, you will recall another piece of correspondence with the same name. Reference to the E folder in the file drawer shows that although the names are the same, these are two different people who live on different streets. Therefore, you will need to code additional units beyond the name to determine the correct alphabetic order.

#20:   All invoices are filed in a separate subject folder. The word *Invoice* appears on the invoice form; however, the actual folder label is INVOICES. Underline the word *Invoice* at the top right of the form and add an *s* to the word. *Invoices* is the key unit. The second and succeeding units in the filing segment are the name of the company to whom the invoice is sent: *1* is the second unit, *Way* is the third unit, and *Direct* is the fourth unit. Keep the invoice with your other coded pieces.

#22:   This piece is another invoice. Code as you did for piece #20.

#24:   Prepare a cross-reference for the full name for this business: Chicago Technology, Inc. The correspondence address uses the popular name. Be sure to write 24X at the bottom right of the cross-reference sheet.

#25:   This outgoing letter is in response to #17. At the top right of the letter, write the English translation of the foreign business name. Code the translation. There is no need to prepare a cross-reference sheet for this piece because you prepared one for piece #17.

#26:   Prepare two cross-reference sheets for this compound business name.

#28:   Note the special instruction from TW; prepare an individual folder as you did for piece #17. The contents of this letter indicate a name change for a company with which Auric Systems, Inc. has been doing business for years. Rather than go back through all previous correspondence and change the coded name, a permanent cross-reference should be prepared. Use a blank cross-reference sheet. At the top of the sheet, under Name or Subject, write the new name of the company and code it (99 Electronic Repair Shop). After SEE, below Name or Subject, write the former name of the company (Adams Electronic Repairs). Leave the Date of Record and Regarding lines blank. For reporting purposes, write 6 after Job No. and 28X after Cross-Reference No. This sheet will always be the first item in the 99 ELECTRONIC REPAIR SHOP folder. In an actual office, you would place the permanent cross-reference sheet at the beginning of the records for the former name and add a SEE line to the label of the folder with the former name.

#29:   This letter is from the State of Illinois Communications Commission—a state government agency.

5. Sort your coded pieces into eight piles (NUMBERS through I) and then separate the individual folders from the other coded pieces. File the individual folders behind the appropriate guides in the file drawer. Then file the coded pieces in each pile in the proper folders with the pieces filed in Job 5. Check to see that individual folders and special guides and folders precede the general folder in each section.

6. Examine the contents of the general folders to determine if three or more pieces have accumulated for any one correspondent. If so, prepare the necessary folders and move the correspondence pieces from the general folders to the new folders. File the new folders in the correct order in your file drawer.

7. Complete Report Sheet 6. Start at the *bottom* of each column as you indicate the order of the pieces. List cross-references with an X and unreleased pieces with a check mark. Keep your file drawer intact.

8. Check your report sheet as your instructor directs.

9. If necessary, rearrange and recode any items that were incorrectly filed. You will add items to your file drawer in Job 7. If your instructor directs, take Finding Test 6.

Computer Activity

In this activity, you will continue to record names and addresses for contacts who correspond with the company in the *Access* database.

1. Locate the *Access* file *Job 5 Contacts* that you updated in Job 5. Make a copy of the file and name it *Job 6 Contacts*. Open the *Job 6 Contacts* file.

2. Enter the names and addresses from correspondence pieces 16 to 30 into the appropriate table. Follow the guidelines given in Job 5 when entering records. Sales invoices (Piece 20) are sent to customers. Enter **Customer** in the Category field for records for sales invoices. Remember to create only one record for each correspondent, even if there are two or more pieces of correspondence to or from the correspondent. You may have entered records for some correspondents in Job 5. Update records entered earlier if more information (such as a title) is provided on the new piece of correspondence.

3. Run the **Category Query** and print the query results table.

4. In the Category query results, how many records have "Customer" in the category field?

5. In the Category query results, how many records have "Other" in the category field?

6. In the Contacts table, how many vendors are located in Northbrook?

Care of Supplies

Keep the guides, folders, and correspondence pieces intact in your file drawer. You will add more items to the file drawer in Job 7. If labels for other jobs are on the same sheet as Job 6 labels, store the sheet of labels in the Supplies 1 Envelope for later use.

Job 7

Correspondence Filing—Rules 1–10 and Tickler File Usage

Although you have been aware of the tickler file notations that appear on many of the pieces of correspondence, you have not had the responsibility for making the tickler file entries until this time. In this job, your objectives are to apply the ten rules of alphabetic filing and to learn tickler file usage.

Supplies Needed

- File drawer with guides, folders, and correspondence pieces filed correctly as a result of Jobs 5 and 6
- 1 one-fifth cut, second position, preprinted guide (Supplies 1 Envelope): CHICAGO
- 1 one-third cut, third position, preprinted folder (Supplies 1 Envelope): CHICAGO
- 2 one-fifth cut, first position, preprinted tickler file guides (Supplies 1 Envelope): MARCH and APRIL
- 6 one-fifth cut, second position, preprinted tickler file guides (Supplies 1 Envelope): 1–5, 6–10, 11–15, 16–20, 21–25, and 26–31
- 16 correspondence pieces numbered 31 through 45 (Forms Pad 3)
- 3 cross-reference sheets (Forms Pad 3)
- 8 blank cards for use in the tickler file (Forms Pad 4)
- Report Sheet 7 (Data CD)
- Pencil

File Setup

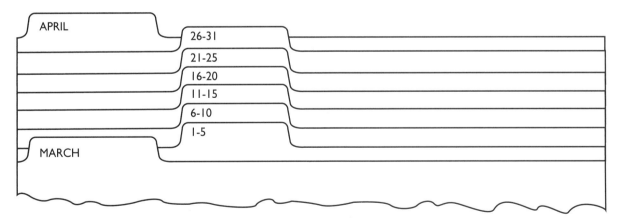

Place the two monthly guides and the six daily guides in the front of your file drawer as shown in the above illustration. To save space, dates have been combined into groups of five. A tickler file actually in use would have a separate guide for each day.

General Information

When information must be called to someone's attention at a future date, some type of reminder is prepared to note the information needed on that date. The reminder is filed under that date in a chronological file most often known as a **tickler file.** In this job, you will use blank cards to prepare the necessary reminders for correspondence pieces 31 through 45.

When someone releases a letter for filing, that person may make notations on the letter pertaining to answering the letter or a date when the letter should be brought to that person's attention again. Filers, too, as they prepare records for filing, scan the contents to see if a tickler notation is needed. If it is, the filer writes the tickler file date on the record and prepares a tickler entry before filing.

The first correspondence piece for which you must prepare a tickler file entry is #34. Pat Johnson has written a note requesting a reminder to check this order on March 1. Information in the tickler entry must include the following:

Date   When is the record wanted or a reminder needed?

Who   Who wants the reminder?

Why   Why is the reminder wanted (the date of a scheduled meeting or event is near, a special offer is about to expire, an order is expected, and so on)?

Related Record   What name is the related record filed under and what is the date of the record?

For the purposes of this simulation, the number of the correspondence piece should be written in the upper right corner of the tickler card for listing on the report sheet. As is often done in an office, you may write the information on the cards instead of keying it. Be sure your writing is legible and that you use consistent format and spacing. Below is an illustration of the tickler card for #34.

March 1   34
Remind Pat Johnson to check on an order. RG-6, RG-8, and
RG-59 cables have been ordered.
All State Cable Inc dated 2/20/—

The tickler card for #34 will be placed in the 1–5 date section behind the MARCH guide in the tickler file. The letter, of course, will be filed in its proper place in the correspondence file. If a tickler card is made for a month other than the current month, that card is placed behind the appropriate monthly guide and redistributed on the first day of that month to its proper daily guide.

Filing Procedures

1. Carefully remove correspondence pieces numbered 31 through 45 from Forms Pad 3.

2. Remove three cross-reference sheets from Forms Pad 3 and place them at the front of your file drawer.

3. Remove eight blank cards from Forms Pad 4 and place them in front of the cross-reference sheets at the front of your file drawer.

4. Inspect each piece of correspondence to see if it has been released for filing. If a record does not bear a release mark, place a check mark next to the piece number on the record, as you have done before.

5. Code each piece for filing. Consult the indexing and cross-referencing rules, the following comments, or your instructor if you encounter any difficulties.

   #34: Prepare a tickler card as shown on page 42. As you prepare the tickler cards, place them in a pile separate from the correspondence pieces. This name could also be written as Allstate; prepare a SEE ALSO cross-reference.

   #35: 007 Spy Channel is a division of Imagine! Films, Inc. Prepare a cross-reference sheet for the parent company name. Note also Pat Johnson's written request and prepare a tickler card.

   #37: There is no written note with this tickler file notation. Read the letter to determine what the reminder should be, then prepare a tickler card.

   #38: Prepare a tickler card from PJ's written notation.

   #39: Prepare a tickler card based on the contents of the letter.

   #41: Prepare a tickler card based on the contents of the letter.

   #42: Prepare a tickler card based on the contents of the letter. Disregard the destruction notation at this time.

   #44: Prepare a tickler card based on the contents of the letter.

6. As you coded the correspondence, you prepared the necessary cards for the tickler file. File those cards in the tickler file now. Remember that in this job you are to assume you are working with the tickler file during the month of March. Therefore, place tickler cards with March dates behind the daily guides. The order of the cards behind any one daily guide is with the earliest date first. For example, behind the 11–15 guide, a card dated March 13 would be placed in front of a card dated March 14. Place cards bearing April dates behind the APRIL guide in chronological order to be distributed at the beginning of April behind the proper daily guides.

7. After you have finished filing the tickler cards, sort your coded pieces into piles (NUMBERS through I) and separate any pieces to be filed in individual folders from the other coded pieces. You will notice many pieces with the key unit of *Chicago*. To aid retrieval of these pieces, adding a CHICAGO special guide and a CHICAGO special folder seems wise.

8. Remove the CHICAGO special guide from the Supplies 1 Envelope. Behind this guide there must be a correspondingly labeled folder. Remove the CHICAGO special folder from the Supplies 1 Envelope. Place the guide and folder behind the C primary guide. The folder will contain all pieces with a key unit of *Chicago.*

9. Further sort the C pile into two piles: one for the pieces with a key unit of Chicago, and one for the pieces with a key unit that starts with C.

10. File the Chicago pieces in alphabetic order in the CHICAGO special folder. All correspondence with a Chicago key unit should be stored in this new CHICAGO special folder. Therefore, examine the contents of the C general folder for pieces with a key unit of Chicago. Remove those pieces from the C general folder and file them in the CHICAGO special folder in alphabetic order with the other Chicago pieces.

11. File any individual folders behind the appropriate guides in the file drawer. Then, file the remaining coded pieces in the proper folders with the pieces filed in Jobs 5 and 6. Jog the folders, if necessary, to straighten the edges of the pieces for a neat-looking file.

12. Examine the contents of the general folders to determine if three or more pieces of correspondence with identical coding have accumulated.

13. List on Report Sheet 7 the contents of your correspondence file (note check marks for unreleased records). Also list on Report Sheet 7 the contents of your tickler file.

14. Check your report sheet as your instructor directs.

15. Be sure that you understand any misfilings that may have occurred. Recode and rearrange any items that were incorrectly filed so that your correspondence file is in the correct order. You will use these pieces again in Jobs 8 and 9. If your instructor directs, take Finding Test 7.

Computer Activity
Part 1 Database Records

In this activity, you will continue to record names and addresses for contacts who correspond with the company in the *Access* database.

1. Locate the *Access* file *Job 6 Contacts* that you updated in Job 6. Make a copy of the file and name it *Job 7 Contacts.* Open the *Job 7 Contacts* file.

2. Enter the names and addresses from correspondence pieces 31 to 45 into the appropriate table. Follow the guidelines given in Jobs 5 and 6 when entering records. Remember to create only one record for each correspondent.

3. Run the **Category Query** and print the query results table.

4. Create a report to display data for job applicants. Base the report on the Applicants table. Include all fields in the report. Choose **Columnar** for the layout. Save the report as **Applicants Report.** Print the report.

5. In the Contacts table, how many records are for contacts outside the United States?

6. In the Contacts table, how many records are for contacts in U.S. states other than IL?

7. In the Applicants table, what is the street address for Chris Carter?

Part 2 Tickler File

1. Launch your application software, such as *Microsoft Outlook,* which has a calendar feature.

2. Beginning at the front of your file drawer, examine each piece of correspondence for a tickler notation. For correspondence pieces with a tickler notation, enter tickler information to appear on the calendar in the appropriate month (next March or April).

   As for a manual tickler file, indicate the following information:

   Date Enter the reminder on the appropriate date when the reminder or record is needed. If your software requires you to enter a time for each item on the calendar, use 9:00 a.m. as the time for reminders that have only a date and no specific time attached.

   Who Key **Tickler** and the initials of a person who wants the reminder. For example, key Tickler PJ to indicate that a tickler item is a reminder for Pat Johnson.

   Why Indicate why the reminder is wanted (the date of a scheduled meeting or event is near, a special offer is about to expire, an order is expected, and so on).

   Related Record Key the name the related record is filed under (in indexing order) and the date of the record. For the purposes of this simulation, key the record number in parentheses at the end of the reminder.

   A sample tickler entry in *Microsoft Outlook* for piece no. 35 is shown in the illustration on page 46.

3. Save and print the tickler entries.

Care of Supplies

Keep the correspondence section of your file drawer intact; you will use this file arrangement in Job 8. Remove the tickler file from the front of the file drawer. Store the guides in the Supplies 2 Envelope. Discard the tickler file cards.

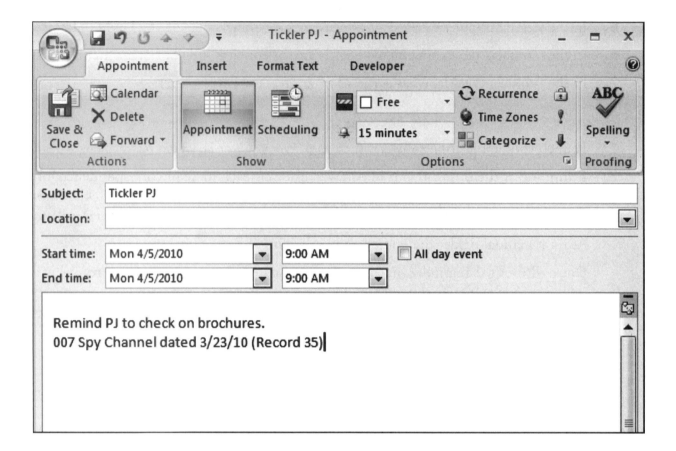

Job 8

Requisition and Charge-Out Procedures

The objectives of this job are to give you practice in finding records requested from the files, charging those records to the persons requesting them, and following up on those records. The use of OUT sheets is emphasized.

Supplies Needed

- File drawer with all records (1 through 45) filed correctly as a result of Job 7
- 10 OUT sheets (Forms Pad 4)
- Report Sheet 8/Charge-Out Log (Data CD)
- Pencil

General Information

As records manager, you receive all requests for records from the files. These requests come from the persons or departments by written note, orally by telephone or in person, and on the requisition form (OUT sheet) used by Auric Systems, Inc. Your procedure upon receiving a request is as follows:

1. a. If the request comes by written requisition (an OUT sheet), locate the desired record, check the OUT sheet for completeness, and add whatever information is necessary.
    b. If the request is oral, locate the record and complete a requisition form (OUT sheet).
    c. If the request is by note, not on a requisition form, locate the record and complete a requisition form (OUT sheet).

2. Record on the Charge-Out Log (Report Sheet 8) the information that is asked regarding the requested record. Keep the Charge-Out Log on your desk for follow-up purposes.

3. Remove the requested record from the folder and replace it with the requisition form (the OUT sheet). You may remove the complete contents of a folder if such a request has been made, but do not remove the folder itself. In an actual situation, you would send the record to the person who requested it. For this job, you may store the requested records at the front of your file drawer.

4. Since all borrowed records should be returned to the files within a certain time period (usually one week), the date the records are to be returned should be indicated in the Date Due column on the Charge-Out Log for follow-up purposes. If someone requests an extension of time for borrowing a record and no one else has requested the record, fill out the Extended Date Due column and change the date that the record is to be returned on the OUT sheet.

5. When a borrowed record is returned to you, refile it in the appropriate folder, remove the OUT sheet, and set it aside for checking purposes. Write the date the record was returned in the Date Returned column on the Charge-Out Log.

6. If a borrowed record is not returned by the date due, you would call or send a notice to the person or department that borrowed the record. The borrower's phone number is listed in the Ext. No. column on the Charge-Out log. The date of the overdue notice is recorded on the Charge-Out Log in the Date Overdue Notice Sent column (with "called" noted if that method of notification was used). A new due date of one week later than the original due date is recorded in the Extended Date Due column and on the OUT sheet.

Filing Procedures

1. Print the *Word* file *Report Sheet 8* found in the data files. You will make entries on this Charge-Out Log as you work through Job 8.

2. Remove OUT sheets numbered 1 through 10 from Forms Pad 4. The OUT sheets are numbered in the upper left corner; keep them in numeric order. OUT Sheet 1 has been completed for you as a guide.

3. The events that occurred from March 5 to March 27 are given below. As you work, be very careful to remember these dates in relation to the pieces of correspondence. Your file contains pieces dated after that time period (that would not have been filed at that time). Use the OUT sheets in numeric order for the list of events so that you can keep an accurate record of events as they occur.

Take whatever action is required by (a) completing OUT sheets, (b) making notations on the Charge-Out Log of records borrowed, and (c) following up to see that the borrowed records are returned within one week. As you remove OUT sheets from your file folders, set them aside for checking purposes later.

a. On March 5 you receive an OUT sheet from Pat Johnson (Ext. 5695). Locate the requested record. Check to see that all necessary information appears on the OUT sheet. OUT Sheet 1 has been completed as an example. Normally, you would fill in the date the record is due (3/12—one week from the date the record was borrowed) and write the record number (3) after Record No. Complete the Charge-Out Log. (All information for OUT Sheet 1 has been entered on the Charge-Out Log as an example for you to follow.) Remove the record from the folder and replace it with OUT Sheet 1. Place the record at the front of your file drawer as a substitute for delivering it to Pat Johnson.

b. On March 9, Pat Johnson comes to your desk and says: "Please get me the invoice that we sent to 2001 Systems, Inc. sometime last month." Locate the record, prepare OUT Sheet 2, and complete the Charge-Out Log. Remove the record and replace it with the OUT sheet. Place the record at the front of the file drawer.

c. Also on March 9, Glen Norris (Ext. 5235) phones you and asks for the letter from Airwaves Extra-ordinary! regarding their representative Jessica Allen. Locate the record, prepare OUT Sheet 3, and complete the Charge-Out Log. Remove the record and insert the OUT sheet. Place the record at the front of the file drawer where borrowed records are accumulating.

d. On March 10, Pat Johnson returns the letter she borrowed on March 5. Remove the letter from the front of the file drawer and refile it in proper order. Remove the OUT sheet and set it aside. Complete the Date Returned column of the Charge-Out Log.

e. On March 13, Pat Johnson calls and says: "I would like the copy of our invoice to 21st Century Networks in Skokie, IL, just as quickly as you can get it to me, please." Locate the record, prepare OUT Sheet 4, and complete the Charge-Out Log. Remove the record and file the OUT sheet.

f. On March 16, Glen Norris calls and asks to keep the letter from Airwaves Extra-Ordinary! for another week. Make the necessary changes on the Charge-Out Log and on the OUT Sheet.

g. On March 16, Terri Williams (Ext. 5316) asks for the letter written by the engineers who are testing the larger size fiber optic tubing. She thinks the name is Davis Engineers. Locate the record, complete OUT Sheet 5, and make the necessary entries on your Charge-Out Log. Remove the record and file the OUT sheet.

h. On March 17, you check your Date Due column and notify anyone who needs to be reminded to return records to the file. Make the necessary notations on your Charge-Out Log and on the OUT sheet(s). (You need not actually complete a notification form.)

i. On March 18, Glen Norris returns the letter he borrowed on March 9. Remove the letter from the front of the file drawer and refile it in proper order. Remove the OUT sheet and set it aside.

j. On March 18, Terri Williams asks you for the "letter from the person who applied for a CSR job around the first of March. I think her name was Chris Carter."

k. On March 19, Pat Johnson requests the correspondence that has been filed *to date* concerning Above & Beyond Insurance Co.

l. On March 19, Terri Williams returns the letter from Burns, Davis, and Isaacson, Engineers.

m. On March 19, Terri Williams sends OUT Sheet 8 for the letter indicated. Check the OUT sheet for completeness.

n. On March 20, Pat Johnson asks to keep the 21st Century Networks invoice another week.

o. On March 20, Glen Norris asks you for the copy of our letter to DeTemple Internet Supplier in Skokie, IL.

p. On March 22, Pat Johnson asks you for the letter written by Dean Charles Ingersol, Chicago School of the Arts.

q. On March 23, Pat Johnson returns the 2001 Systems, Inc. invoice.

r. On March 26, Terri Williams returns the letter from Gene Jenewein of the Chicago Broadband Association.

s. On March 26, you check the Date Due column and send notifications where necessary.

t. On March 27, Terri Williams returns the application letter written by Chris Carter.

u. On March 27, you check the Date Due column and send notifications where necessary.

4. Check your Charge-Out Log (Report Sheet 8) to be certain all of the events have been properly recorded.

5. Give to your instructor:

a. All OUT sheets that have been completed and removed from the file, arranged in numeric order. Do not remove any OUT sheets from your file drawer.

b. The records borrowed but not returned, also arranged in numeric order (taken from the front of your file drawer).

c. Report Sheet 8.

d. Your correspondence file drawer. Place your name on the file drawer and on each group of records submitted for 5a through 5c above.

6. Job 8 does not have a Finding Test.

Computer Activity

In this activity, you will create a new *Access* database to keep track of charge-out data electronically.

1. Create a new blank *Access* database. Name the file *Job 8 Charge Log.*

2. Create a new table named **Charge Log.** Create the following fields in the table: Record ID, Name on Record, Record Date, Borrower, Phone Ext, Date Borrowed, Date Due, Date Returned, Overdue Notice Sent, and Extended Due Date. Make the Record ID field a number field. Make all other fields text fields. Make the Record ID field the primary key.

3. Enter the data you recorded on Report Sheet 8, Charge-Out Log, into the database table. Enter the Record No. in the Record ID field. Use the current year in dates. Use leading zeros as needed so that all dates have the same number of digits (example: 03/09/2010) to facilitate sorting. Note that two records should be entered for OUT Sheet 7.

4. Create a query to show a list of records that have been borrowed but not yet returned. Base the query on the Charge Log table. Show the Record ID, Record Date, Name on Record, Borrower, and Phone Ext fields in the query results. Include but do not show the Date Returned field. Enter **Is Null** in the Criteria row for the Date Returned field. Sort the results by the Name on Record field. Name the query **OUT Records.** Print the query results.

5. Create a query to display records for which overdue notices have been sent. Base the query on the Charge Log table. Show the Record ID, Record Date, Name on Record, Borrower, and Overdue Notice Sent fields in the query results. Enter an asterisk (*) in the Criteria row for the Overdue Notice Sent field. Sort the results by the Name on Record field. Name the query **Notices Sent.** Print the query results.

6. How many records have been borrowed and not yet returned?

7. Who borrowed the document with Record ID 21?

8. To whom was an overdue notice sent for the Invoices 2001 Systems, Inc. record?

Care of Supplies

After all materials have been returned to you, remove the remaining OUT sheets and replace all records in their correct folders in the file drawer for use in Job 9. Discard all OUT sheets.

Job 9

Transfer Procedures

The objective of this job is to learn to control the volume of records in your file containers by transferring records to inactive storage. In many offices, transfer takes place at a stated time of the year. Auric Systems, Inc. has chosen to do this work at the end of the first quarter when business activity is lightest. Therefore, you are to assume that you are transferring records in April.

Supplies Needed

- File drawer with all records filed correctly as a result of Job 7
- Report Sheet 9 (Data CD)
- Pencil

General Information

Auric Systems, Inc. uses a periodic transfer method that is described in Chapter 7 of the textbook, RECORDS MANAGEMENT, Ninth Edition. The periodic transfer method moves records from active storage to inactive storage at the end of a stated period of time. Businesses usually schedule transfer times at points when business activity is lowest so that the day-to-day operations of the business are not affected by the transfer process. In some companies, all departments transfer inactive records at one time. Other companies select different time periods for the various departments to transfer inactive records. In either case, the records transfer procedure should be performed on a regular basis.

In an actual office, records of the current year, called active records, are kept in the file folders in active storage. Records of the previous year(s) are kept in similarly labeled folders in inactive storage (sometimes in the same type of storage equipment and sometimes at another location). Although you will transfer records from active to inactive storage, to save time, you will not prepare the new folders that would be required. Cross-reference sheets are transferred according to their dates as well.

You can assume that previous inactive records have been transferred to archive storage or destroyed according to the retention and destruction schedule of Auric Systems, Inc. This transfer has made room for the records you will now transfer from active to inactive storage.

You will note that the records with which you have been working bear February, March, and April dates. February and March are last quarter, and April is the current quarter.

Transfer Guidelines for Auric Systems, Inc.

1. Transfer takes place as soon as possible after March 31.

2. If all records in an individual folder bear February and March dates only, the entire folder is transferred to inactive storage.

3. If some of the records in an individual folder are dated last quarter and some are dated this quarter, the folder and all its contents remain in the active files.

4. All special folders remain in the active files. In special folders, records bearing February and March dates are transferred to the inactive files; records bearing April dates remain in the special folder in active storage. If records for the same correspondent are mixed (some are dated first quarter and some are dated this quarter), they all remain in the active file.

5. All general folders remain in the active files. In general folders, these transfer possibilities exist:
    a. If records for the same correspondent are all dated prior to April 1, the records are transferred to inactive storage.
    b. If records for the same correspondent are all dated April 1 or thereafter, they remain in the active files.
    c. If records for the same correspondent are mixed (some are dated last quarter and some are dated this quarter), they all remain in the active files.

6. If a record has a special notation to destroy or transfer at a certain time, follow that instruction. (However, do not actually destroy any piece. You will need it in succeeding jobs. Place records to be destroyed at the front of your file drawer.)

7. If the contents of a record refer to something that will happen on or after April 1, leave that record in the active files even if it is dated last quarter. #35 is the first record of this type you will encounter.

8. A tickler notation with an April date indicates that the record needs to be retained in the active files.

9. Transfer cross-reference sheets according to the Date of Record. Cross-references bearing February and March dates are transferred to the inactive file (unless the cross-reference refers to a record or records retained in the active file for some reason). Cross-references bearing April dates remain in active storage. Cross-references bearing no date are permanent SEE ALSO cross-references and are retained in the active files.

These guidelines are very important. Read them again to be sure you understand them thoroughly. Guidelines 7 and 8 are particularly important; you will need to skim the contents of each record as you contemplate its transfer. Refer constantly to these guidelines to refresh your memory as you work.

Transfer Procedures

1. Check your file drawer to be sure all records removed in Job 8 have been refiled in their correct folders.

2. Inspect the contents of each folder, beginning at the front of the file drawer and working to the back. Follow Guidelines 2 and 3 if you are inspecting an individual folder. Follow Guideline 4 if you are inspecting a special folder. Follow Guideline 5 if you are in specting a general folder. Guideline 6 applies to special notations on correspondence. Guidelines 7 and 8 apply to all records—retain in the active files the records you will be working with regularly. Guideline 9 applies to cross-reference sheets.

3. As you find records that are to be transferred to inactive storage, remove them and place them face down in a stack on your desk. The records will be in alphabetic order in case a request comes in for a record dated last quarter. In an actual office, you would prepare a folder with the same label as the one from which you removed the records to be transferred. You would use the old folder for transfer and place the new folder in the active files to hold the active records. To save time, this step is omitted—you need not prepare new folders. If you find that the entire contents of an individual folder should be transferred, remove the entire folder and lay it face down in a stack on your desk.

4. If you are interrupted in your work, pick up the stack you have been accumulating and carefully place those records (and any folders) in the back of the drawer, facing away from you. All of your transferred records will be stored behind your active files facing in the opposite direction. As you work with your active files, you cannot read the inactive records; active files face one way and inactive files face the other.

5. When you have finished transferring records, complete Report Sheet 9. Beginning at the *bottom* of the report sheet, list the label captions of the folders that remain in your active file. Then list the piece numbers of the records remaining in those active folders across from the folder name, including any cross-reference sheets. Also list on Report Sheet 9 the piece numbers of the destroyed records.

6. Check your work as your instructor directs. When your work has been checked, correct any errors you may have made. Be sure you understand why your report sheet was incorrect. Job 9 does not have a Finding Test.

Computer Activity

1. Open the Inbox folder on the data disk. This folder contains simulated e-mail messages sent to you, the Records Manager.

2. Open each file; scan its contents and note the date of the message.

3. Follow the general guidelines below for managing e-mail. (List the names of the files that should be deleted without actually deleting the files.)

   a. Delete any e-mail message that is over 30 days old. (Assume the current date is April 8.)

   b. Delete any e-mail message when the task it describes has been completed or a deadline mentioned has passed.

   c. Retain other e-mail messages.

4. Open the Outbox folder on the data disk. This folder contains simulated e-mail messages sent by you.

5. Open each file; scan its contents and note the date of the message.

6. Follow the guidelines listed in Step 3 to determine whether to keep or delete the message.

7. Create a list of e-mail files to be retained in the Inbox folder and a list of e-mail files to be deleted from the Inbox folder.

8. Create a list of e-mail files to be retained in the Outbox folder and a list of e-mail files to be deleted from the Outbox folder. Submit your lists as your instructor directs.

9. Should the Inbox file *Ingrahm Appt* be retained or deleted? Why?

10. When is the report on the services offered by Elite, Inc. due to Pat Johnson?

11. What is the name of the employee for whom a reference check is requested in an Outbox message?

Care of Supplies

1. Remove all contents of your file drawer. Put the records in numeric order, 1 through 45, for use in Job 10.

2. Place the one-fifth cut, first position guides in the Supplies 2 Envelope.

3. Place the one-fifth cut, second position guides in the Supplies 2 Envelope.

4. Place all one-third cut, third position folders in the Supplies 2 Envelope.

5. Discard all used cross-reference sheets.

Job 10

Subject Correspondence Filing

The objective of this job is to file records correctly by subject. You will work with a subject index that has already been prepared to determine in which subject category records belong.

Supplies Needed

- File drawer
- Correspondence pieces 1 through 45 (used previously)
- 2 one-fifth cut, first position preprinted guides (Supplies 1 Envelope): ADMINISTRATION and CUSTOMER
- 6 one-third cut, third position, blank folders (Supplies 1 Envelope)
- Sheet containing self-adhesive labels for Job 10 (Supplies 1 Envelope)
- Report Sheet 10 (Data CD)
- Pencil

File Setup

1. From the Supplies 1 Envelope, remove the two one-fifth cut, first position guides labeled: ADMINISTRATION and CUSTOMER

2. Place the guides in your file drawer in alphabetic order. These guides are the main subject primary guides.

3. Remove six blank one-third cut, third position folders from the Supplies 1 Envelope.

4. Remove the sheet containing labels for Job 10 from the Supplies 1 Envelope. Affix the following labels to five of the blank folders:

   AAP ADMINISTRATION ADVERTISING AND PUBLICITY
   AAS ADMINISTRATION APPLICATIONS
   AGR ADMINISTRATION GOVERNMENT REGULATIONS
   CIN CUSTOMER INVOICES
   CIQ CUSTOMER INQUIRIES

   These folders are the main and subdivision subject general folders. At this point, there will be one folder without a label; place it at the back of your file drawer for use as needed.

5. Place each labeled folder behind its correspondingly labeled guide in your file drawer.

6. Check the order of your guides and folders with the illustration shown on the following page.

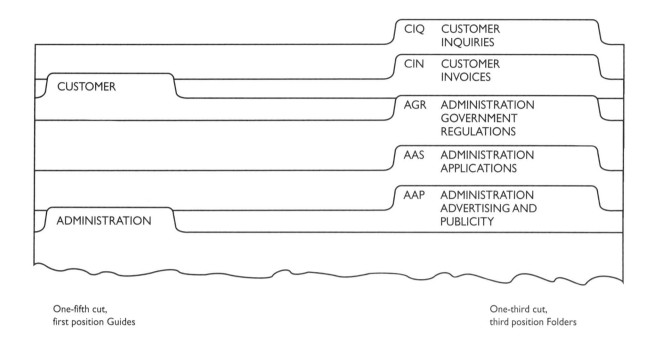

One-fifth cut,
first position Guides

One-third cut,
third position Folders

7. Place the 45 correspondence pieces in numeric order in the front of your file drawer. You will be instructed later which pieces to use in this job.

General Information

When filing according to a subject method, you must be thoroughly familiar with the subjects to be used. Carefully study the following subject index so that you know the main subjects under which records are to be filed.

Each main subject has subdivisions. Study them carefully, too, so that you are familiar with them. Note that the labels have three-letter codes at the beginning. Research has shown that using coded labels reduces the number of misfiles.

No other subjects or subdivisions of subjects are to be added to this list. All the records with which you will be working will fit into one of the categories listed.

SUBJECT INDEX

ADMINISTRATION

      AAP   ADMINISTRATION ADVERTISING AND PUBLICITY

      AAS   ADMINISTRATION APPLICATIONS

      AGR   ADMINISTRATION GOVERNMENT REGULATIONS

CUSTOMER

      CIN   CUSTOMER INVOICES

      CIQ   CUSTOMER INQUIRIES

Filing Procedures—General

1. Although you have previously scanned the contents of each of the records with which you will now be working, reread each one carefully to determine the subject that corresponds to one of the subject titles listed in your subject index.

2. After you have determined the subject of the record, clearly write the three-letter code for that subject in the upper right corner of the piece. Underline the three-letter code for the key unit. The three-letter code is the key unit on the file folder label. For example, if a letter is from or to a customer about an inquiry, write *CIQ* in the upper right corner and underline it. The correspondent name completes the filing segment.

3. Arrange the pieces of correspondence in a subject folder according to the names of the correspondents. Follow the rules used in the alphabetic filing method. If two pieces concern one correspondent, place the piece with the most recent date in front.

4. When three pieces concerning the same correspondent have accumulated in a subject folder, prepare an individual folder for that correspondent. If instructions to open an individual folder appear on any of the records, be sure to do so immediately. *The label on an individual folder should always bear the three-letter subject code, the main subject name, the subject subdivision name, and the correspondent's name.*

5. Disregard any tickler file notations that appear on any of the letters.

6. As you code, rough sort the records to avoid handling them twice (once for coding purposes and once for sorting). Accumulate stacks on your desk according to the two main subjects.

Filing Procedures—Specific

1. Remove the 45 correspondence pieces from the front of your file drawer. Select the following records, keeping them in numeric order: 5, 6, 7, 11, 15, 19, 20, 21, 22, 27, 29, 37, 38, 39, and 43. Check your selections to be sure you have the correctly numbered records with which to work. Place the correspondence pieces not selected in the front of the file drawer.

2. Code the records for subject filing. Coding instructions for the first seven pieces follow. Coding that has been done previously is still needed, as those names complete the subject filing segments.

   #5:   This application letter should be filed under AAS ADMINISTRATION APPLICATIONS. Code the letter AAS (remember to underline the three-letter code) and sort it into a stack for Administration records to be filed later.

   #6:   This letter is a customer inquiry. Write the code for CUSTOMER INQUIRIES (CIQ) in the upper right corner and sort the letter into a Customer stack.

   #7:   This letter is a special offer for various cable channels. Write the code for ADMINISTRATION ADVERTISING AND PUBLICITY (AAP) in the upper right corner and sort the letter into the Administration stack.

#11:   This letter is in response to #6. Write the code CIQ in the upper right corner and sort the letter into the Customer stack.

#15:   This letter is the third piece of correspondence concerning Above & Beyond Insurance Co. Code the letter (CIQ) and sort it into the Customer stack.

#19:   This letter is a customer inquiry. Code the letter (CIQ) and sort it into the Customer stack.

#20:   This customer invoice is for wireless phones. Write the code for CUSTOMER INVOICES (CIN) in the upper right corner and sort the invoice into the Customer stack.

3. Continue reading records #21 through #29 and determine the proper subject category by which to file each one. Write the subject code at the top right of each record and sort each record into its proper stack for filing later.

   The following comments will be helpful to you as you code #21 through #29:

   #21:   This letter is advertising a workshop Auric Systems, Inc. is hosting. This is Advertising and Publicity.

   #22 and #27:   Each of these records is a customer invoice.

   #29:   This letter is about new State of Illinois regulations. Code it ADMINISTRA-TION GOVERNMENT REGULATIONS (AGR).

4. Before coding any more records, check your work as your instructor directs. Then file in the following sequence:
   a.   File the records in the Administration stack in their correctly labeled folders.
   b.   Continue by filing the records in the Customer stack. Within each folder, the pieces are arranged alphabetically by the name of the correspondent (previously coded). If there is more than one piece for any one name, the pieces are filed chronologically—the more recent date in front. Remember to see that records for the same individual or company are filed together, not separated so that some records are in a general folder and some are in an individual folder.
   c.   Check to see if three or more records have accumulated concerning one corre-spondent. If so, prepare an individual folder. Place the records in it, and file the folder in the file drawer. An individual folder precedes the general folder in its section.

5. Check your work carefully with the order list your instructor will supply. Recode and rearrange any records in your file, if necessary. Analyze any misfiles to determine why your order was incorrect. You will add to your file later, and you will want to be sure the first 11 pieces are in the correct order before you continue.

6. Continue coding #37 through #43 and rough sorting the pieces into stacks for later filing. The following comment may be helpful to you:

   #38:   This letter is in response to #19. Code it CIQ.

7. File all sorted records in their proper folders, being careful to check the alphabetic and chronologic order. Follow the filing sequence given in Step 4.

8. Check the contents of your general folders to see if three or more pieces have accumulated concerning any one correspondent. If so, prepare an individual folder, place the records in it, and file it in your file drawer.

9. Complete Report Sheet 10. The folders are listed in order from bottom to top. To the right of each folder name, list the piece numbers of the records in each folder.

10. Check your work as your instructor directs. Recode and rearrange any items in your file, if necessary. Be sure that you understand any misfiles before taking the Finding Test for Job 10.

Computer Activity

In this activity, you will add a field to a database to indicate the subject code for records.

1. Locate the *Access* file *Job 7 Contacts* that you updated in Job 7. Make a copy of the file and name it *Job 10 Contacts.* Open the *Job 10 Contacts* file.

2. Open the Contacts table. Keep the records with ID numbers 6, 7, 19, 20, 21, 22, 27, 29, 37, 39, and 43. Delete all other records from the table. The Contacts table should now contain 11 records.

3. And a new text field named Subject to the table. Enter a three-letter subject code in the Subject field for each record in the database. Use the same subject codes that you used in coding the paper records in this job. You may wish to use an AutoForm to enter the data.

4. Create a query named **Subject Code** based on the Contacts table. Include the ID, Subject, and Company Name fields in the query. Design the query to sort first in ascending order by the Subject field and then in ascending order by the Company Name field.

5. Save the query and print the query results table.

6. In the Subject Code query results, how many records have the subject code "CIN"?

7. What is the subject code for Chicago School of the Arts?

Care of Supplies

When your instructor directs you to do so:

1. Remove the 15 pieces of correspondence from your file drawer.

2. Arrange the correspondence pieces in the original 1 through 45 numeric order for use in Job 11.

3. Remove all guides and folders and place them in the Supplies 2 Envelope.

4. If labels for other jobs are on the same sheet as Job 10 labels, store the sheet of labels in the Supplies 1 Envelope for later use.

Job 11

Consecutive Numeric Correspondence Filing

The objective of this numeric filing job is to give you practice in working with all of the components of a numeric file. You will file selected correspondence pieces using numbered individual folders, general alphabetic folders, an accession log, and an alphabetic card file of all correspondents' names and two subjects.

Supplies Needed

- File drawer
- 4 one-fifth cut, first-position, preprinted guides (Supplies 2 Envelope) (used previously): NUMBERS, A, C, and I
- 3 one-fifth cut, first-position, preprinted guides (Supplies 1 Envelope): NUMBERS, A, and C
- 2 one-fifth cut, second position, preprinted guides (Supplies 1 Envelope): 100 and 104
- 3 one-third cut, third position, preprinted folders (Supplies 2 Envelope) (used previously): NUMBERS, A, and C
- 6 one-third cut, third position folders (Supplies 2 Envelope) (any used previously)
- Correspondence pieces 1 through 45 (used previously)
- 16 printed alphabetic file cards numbered 1 through 16 (Forms Pad 4)
- Sheet containing self-adhesive labels for Job 11 (Supplies 1 Envelope)
- Report Sheet 11/Accession Log (Data CD)
- A separate sheet of paper on which to list the contents of the alphabetic card file
- Pencil

File Setup

1. From the Supplies 2 Envelope, remove the four previously used one-fifth cut, first-position guides labeled NUMBERS, A, C, and I.

2. Place the four guides in alphabetic order, beginning with NUMBERS, in the front of the file drawer. These guides are your alphabetic card file. (In an actual file, all letters of the alphabet would be used.)

3. From the Supplies 1 Envelope, remove the two one-fifth cut, second-position guides labeled 100 and 104. Place these guides behind the card file guides in the file drawer. (In an actual office, you would have two separate files—one for cards and one for correspondence. In this job, both files are in one drawer to save space.)

4. From the Supplies 1 Envelope, remove the three new one-fifth cut, first-position guides labeled NUMBERS, A, and C. From the Supplies 2 Envelope, remove three previously used one-third cut, third position folders labeled NUMBERS, A, and C. Arrange the three guides and the three folders in alphabetic order behind the 100 and 104 guides. Your file drawer arrangement should look like the illustration shown below.

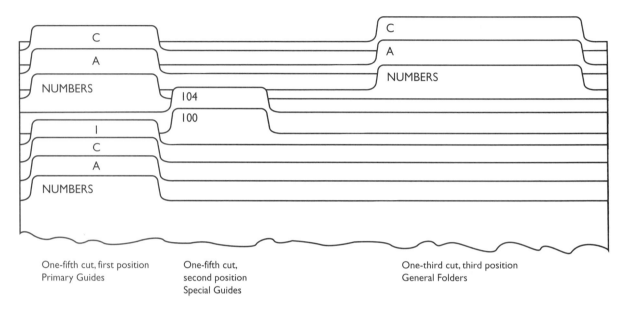

One-fifth cut, first position
Primary Guides

One-fifth cut,
second position
Special Guides

One-third cut, third position
General Folders

5. From the Supplies 2 Envelope, remove any six previously used one-third cut, third-position folders. Remove the sheet containing labels for Job 11 from the Supplies 1 Envelope. Affix the labels with the numbers 100 through 105 carefully on the tabs of the six folders. Place these individual folders in the front of your file drawer where they will be easily accessible as you work.

6. Remove the sixteen printed alphabetic file cards (numbered 1 through 16 in the lower right corners) from Forms Pad 4. Place them in front of you where they will be easily accessible while you are working.

7. Select the following pieces of correspondence, keeping them in numeric order: 2, 5, 6, 11, 13, 15, 17, 19, 20, 22, 25, 35, 36, 37, 38, 39, 41, and 43. Check your selections carefully to be sure you have the correctly numbered records with which to work. Place the selected pieces of correspondence beside the alphabetic file cards in front of you.

8. Because it is not practical to provide a complete accession log for this job, you will use a portion of Report Sheet 11 as an accession log. Print the *Word* file *Report Sheet 11* from the Data CD. Use the section labeled ACCESSION LOG to provide a record of the numbers already assigned and the numbers still available when you need to open a numbered individual folder.

General Information

Two types of file folders are used in a numeric file—those with alphabetic labels and those with numbered labels. An alphabetically arranged card file is always used with a numeric file.

In this job, any correspondent with *two or more pieces* of correspondence is given a numbered individual folder. If a piece of correspondence bears a handwritten note to open an individual folder, a numbered individual folder is prepared immediately. Also, numbered individual folders are prepared for two subjects, applications and invoices. (These instructions differ slightly from those given in previous jobs.)

The first piece to or from any one correspondent is coded with a G in the upper right corner and filed alphabetically by coded name in a *general* alphabetic folder. In an office, you would key the correspondent's name and address on a card to be filed in the alphabetic card file. To save you time, a printed card has been provided for each correspondent, each cross-reference, and for the two subjects. As you code each piece of correspondence with a G in the upper right corner, also code the alphabetic file card with a G in the right corner opposite the keyed name. When a numbered individual folder is assigned, the G is crossed out and the number is written on the correspondence pieces and on the card. Reference is always made to the alphabetic card file before any piece is coded to see if that correspondent's name has already been assigned a number or whether other pieces concerning that correspondent are in the general file.

In numeric filing, cross-references are made for all names that would be cross-referenced in the alphabetic filing method. *Cross-references are in the card file only;* no cross-references are prepared for the correspondence file.

When you code a card for the card file, file it (including any cross-reference cards) immediately in alphabetic order. You may delay filing the correspondence until several pieces have accumulated. Specific directions concerning the filing of correspondence are provided in the next section.

If the pieces of correspondence had not been used in previous jobs, you would need to index and code each piece in the usual manner. Since you have already coded the correspondent name on each piece, you need only skim the piece to refresh your memory of its contents and code each piece with either a G or a folder number (100, 101, etc.) as you proceed. Also, you will need to code any necessary cross-reference cards.

The names of the correspondents who are assigned numbers must be written in an accession log. In this job, use the section labeled ACCESSION LOG on Report Sheet 11 as your accession log.

Filing Procedures

1. At first, the letter G is assigned to each correspondent, except for those for whom a note has been made to open an individual folder. When a *second* piece concerning a correspondent appears, or when a piece is an invoice or applications correspondence, a number is assigned. Following are specific instructions for the first eleven pieces to help you understand the operation of a numeric file.

   #2: Find the file card for Crystal Net Inc, and code it with a G in the upper right corner. File the card behind the C guide in your card file. Code the letter with a G in the upper right corner and place it on your desk to be filed later.

#5:   Applications correspondence is filed in an individual folder because Auric Systems, Inc. is likely to receive more correspondence about that subject. Therefore, APPLICATIONS becomes the first numbered folder in your numeric file. Find the file card prepared for Carter Chris. Reference to your Accession Log shows that number 100 is the next available number to be assigned. Write *Applications* beside that number, then write *100* on the Carter Chris file card in the upper right corner. In your alphabetic card file, you will need a card for Applications, a subject. This is necessary because you may forget what number has been assigned to applications correspondence or someone else may be looking for the applications correspondence and not know the assigned number. Therefore, an Applications card has been prepared; find it and code it 100 also. Write *100* in the upper right corner of correspondence piece #5. File the Applications card behind the A guide and the Carter Chris card behind the C guide in your card file. Remove folder 100 from the front of your file drawer. Place #5 in the folder; file folder 100 behind guide 100 as the first numbered folder in your file.

#6:   Find the file card for Above and Beyond Insurance Co and code it with a G. File the card in the A section of your card file. Code the letter with a G and place it on the pile to be filed later.

#11:   Reference to the card file shows that a card has already been prepared for Above & Beyond Insurance Co. Therefore, an individual folder should be opened because you now have a second piece of correspondence with the same name and address as the first one. Refer to your Accession Log to see that 101 is the next number available for assignment. Write *Above and Beyond Insurance Co* beside 101 on the Accession Log. Change G to 101 on the file card. Refile the card in the card file in correct alphabetic order. Retrieve letter #6 from the unfiled pieces; change the G on it to 101 and code #11 with 101 also. Place both pieces in the 101 folder (the more recent date in front) and file the folder behind the 100 folder in the numeric correspondence file.

#13:   Reference to the card file shows this to be the second letter to or from The Crystal Net, Inc. Refer to your Accession Log for the next number to assign. Write *Crystal Net Inc The* beside 102 on the log. Change G to 102 on the file card for Crystal Net Inc The and refile the card. Retrieve letter #2 from the unfiled pieces; change the G on it to 102 and code #13 with 102. Place both pieces (most recent date in front) in the 102 folder and file the folder behind the 101 folder in the numeric correspondence file.

#15:   This piece is another letter concerning Above & Beyond Insurance Co. Check the card file to see what number has been assigned to Above & Beyond Insurance Co. Code #15 with 101 and place the letter in the 101 folder, most recent date in front.

#17:   This piece bears a handwritten note to open an individual folder. Refer to the Accession Log for the next number to assign. Write *International Computing Center* beside 103 on the log, then write 103 on the file card for International Computing Center. Since there is also a cross-reference file card, find it (Centro de Computacion International) and code it with a 103. File the original card in the I section and the cross-reference card in the C section of your card file. Code the letter with 103, place it in the 103 folder, and file the folder behind the 102 folder in the file drawer.

#19:   Find the card for Chicago School of the Arts. Code the card with a G and file it in the C section of the card file. Code the letter with a G and place it in a pile to be filed later.

#20:   This piece is an invoice, and because Auric Systems, Inc. has so many invoices, they are kept in an individual folder. Write *Invoices* beside the next available number in the Accession Log, which is 104. Find the 1 Way Direct card and code it with 104. Find the Invoices card and code it 104 also. File the 1 Way Direct card in the NUMBERS section of the card file; file the Invoices card in the I section of the card file. Code the invoice with 104, place it in the 104 folder; and file the folder behind the 104 guide.

#22:   Here is another invoice. Since you just worked with an invoice (#20), you know that this invoice (#22) should be coded 104. Find the card, code it, and file it in the proper section of the card file. Code the invoice with 104 and file it in the 104 folder.

#25:   Here is a second letter concerning International Computing Center. Check the card file to see what number has been assigned to International Computing Center. Code #25 and place it in the correct folder, most recent date in front.

2. From this point on, refer to your card file *before* you code each piece to see whether or not that name has been assigned a number or if there is another piece of correspondence already coded.

3. Continue with pieces #35 through #43, checking the card file and either coding with a G or a folder number, or assigning the next number from the Accession Log. Watch for special instructions to open an individual folder and do so. To review, the procedure in assigning a number is as follows:

a.   Beside the next available number on the Accession Log, write the name of the correspondent or subject to whom that number is to be assigned.

b.   Cross out the G on the card and on any cross-reference card that has been filed and write above or next to it the assigned number; refile the cards in the card file.

c.   Retrieve the first piece of correspondence from the general folder or from the pile on your desk and recode it with the assigned number.

d.   Code the second piece of correspondence with the assigned number.

e.   From your supply of numbered individual folders, select the folder labeled with the number assigned to the correspondent.

f.   Place both correspondence pieces in the numbered folder with the more recently dated piece in front.

g.   File the numbered folder in correct numeric sequence in the numeric correspondence section of your file drawer.

4.   After you have coded #43, file your accumulated records.

5.   Carefully check your general folders to see if there is any correspondent with two or more pieces. If there is, a numbered folder should be prepared. You should have already prepared six numbered individual folders (100–105).

6.   Complete the Numeric File Folders and General File Folders sections of Report Sheet 11. List the contents of each folder, beginning at the bottom of each column.

7.   On a separate sheet of paper, report the contents of your card file by listing in alphabetic order the full indexed name on each card and the code assigned to each, such as:

1 Way Direct   104

8.   Submit your report sheet and card file list as your instructor directs. Keep the contents of your file drawer intact. When your work has been checked, recode and rearrange any items in your file drawer, if necessary. Be sure you understand any misfiles before taking Finding Test 11.

Computer Activity

In this activity, you will create an alphabetic index for the records in a numeric filing system.

1.   Create an *Access* file named *Job 11 Index*. Create a new table named **Alphabetic Index.** Create the fields shown below in the table. Make the ID field the primary key.

Field Name	Field Type
ID	Number
Name	Text
File Number	Number

2.   Select the following pieces of correspondence that you used in the manual part of this job: 2, 5, 6, 17, 19, 20, 22, 35, 37, 39, 41, and 43. Enter data for each piece in the database table:

a.   Enter the correspondence piece number in the ID field.

b.   Enter the correspondent's name in the Name field.

c.   Referring to your manual file, enter the number assigned to that piece in the File Number field. If the piece is coded G, enter a **0** (zero) in the File Number field.

3. Sort the table in ascending order by the Name field. Create a report name **Alphabetic Index** to include the Name and File Number fields sorted by the Name field. Print the report.

4. Create a query named **Accession Log** based on the Alphabetic Index table. Include the File Number and Name fields in the query results. Design the query to sort in descending order by the File Number field. Enter **Not 0** in the Criteria row for the File Number field. Run the query and print the query results table.

5. How many records are coded G and do not have an individual file number assigned to them?

6. What file number is assigned to correspondence piece 6?

7. How many records are assigned file number 104?

Care of Supplies

When you are instructed to do so:

1. Remove the pieces of correspondence from the folders and arrange them in the original 1 through 45 numeric order for use in Job 12.

2. Remove the guides and folders from the numeric and general correspondence sections of your file drawer. Place the guides and the folders in the Supplies 2 Envelope.

3. Leave the alphabetic card file guides in your file drawer. Remove the cards but keep them in alphabetic order for use in Job 12.

4. If labels for other jobs are on the same sheet as Job 11 labels, store the sheet of labels in the Supplies 1 Envelope for later use.

Job 12

Terminal-Digit Numeric Correspondence Filing

The objective of this job is to learn the operation of a terminal-digit filing system. Auric Systems, Inc. probably would not use this method to file because it does not have hundreds of thousands of records. By completing this job, however, you will understand the principles involved. Because of space limitations, only a small section of a terminal-digit file will be set up to introduce you to the terminal-digit filing method.

Supplies Needed

- File drawer with card guides used in Job 11: NUMBERS, A, C, and I
- 3 one-fifth cut, first position, card guides (Supplies 2 Envelope) (previously used): B, D, and E
- 2 one-fifth cut, first position guides (any used previously)
- 4 one-fifth cut, second position guides (any used previously)
- 12 one-third cut, third position folders (any used previously)
- Correspondence pieces 1 through 45 (used previously)
- 16 printed alphabetic file cards used in Job 11
- 12 additional printed alphabetic file cards numbered 17 through 28 (Forms Pad 4)
- Sheet containing self-adhesive labels for Job 12 (Supplies 1 Envelope)
- Report Sheet 12/Accession Log (Data CD)
- A separate sheet of paper on which to list the contents of the alphabetic card file
- Colored pencil

General Information

As you know, in the consecutive numbering system, numbers are assigned in order: 700, 701, 702, 703, etc. Therefore, expansion of the file is accomplished by assigning larger numbers. As numbers grow larger, remembering them becomes a problem and misreading easily occurs. As folders are added at the end of the file, activity there could be very heavy. A filer may experience delay in retrieving folders because someone else is working at the files where the most recent folders have been inserted.

To help overcome filers' memory problems and physical congestion at the files, the terminal-digit filing method, an alternative numbering system, can be used. A complete discussion of this method is contained in the textbook, RECORDS MANAGEMENT, Ninth Edition. An abbreviated discussion is given here.

With the terminal-digit numeric method, numbers are assigned to records in the same manner as with the consecutive numeric method—using an accession log and creating an alphabetic name card file. However, there is no general alphabetic section of folders in a terminal-digit file. After a number is assigned to a correspondent (or subject) and coded on a record, a folder is prepared with the same number affixed to its tab as is on the record, and the record is inserted into the folder.

The folder is sorted by reading the number in groups of two or three digits *from right to left.* (In this job you will read the number in groups of two digits.) Remembering to read the number from right to left instead of in the usual manner of reading (left to right) is very important. For example, 810726 is read 26-07-81. The groups of digits are referred to as follows:

26	07	81
Terminal	Secondary	Tertiary
(shelf or drawer)	(guide)	(folder)

The terminal digits usually indicate a drawer or a shelf number. In this example, the drawer number would be 26. The next folder to be filed in the 26 drawer would be labeled 82 07 26, followed by 83 07 26. In the accession log, the numbers are always consecutive; the number following 81 07 26 on the log would be 81 07 27, to be assigned to a folder. Its terminal digit is 27 and that folder would be filed in drawer 27. The next number to be assigned would be 81 07 28 and that numbered folder would be filed in the drawer or on the shelf numbered 28.

In each file drawer, the guide numbers within each terminal-digit section are determined by the numbers of the secondary digits, 00 to 99. The folder is then filed behind its proper guide according to the tertiary number. This procedure is explained in detail later.

In this job, you will use two terminal-digit numbers, identified by two guides with those digits on them (taking the place of separate drawers). You will file records behind each guide in numbered individual folders. Your Accession Log is on Report Sheet 12 and shows the numbers to be assigned. If the Accession Log were complete, it would have thousands of numbers, all consecutively arranged. Only the numbers you will be using are listed on your Accession Log. Print the *Word* file *Report Sheet 12* from the Data CD. The first number on the Accession Log is 20 42 68. If the log were complete, that number would be followed by 20 42 69, 20 42 70, 20 42 71, etc. Understanding that this log has been abbreviated for your use is very important.

File Setup

1. The alphabetic card file guides used in Job 11 (NUMBERS, A, C, and I) remain in your file drawer. Remove the NUMBERS guide and place it in the Supplies 2 Envelope. Remove previously used guides B, D, and E from the Supplies 2 Envelope and place them in your file drawer in alphabetic order. This is your alphabetic card file.

2. Remove the sheet containing labels for Job 12 from the Supplies 1 Envelope. Affix labels 67 and 68 to any two previously used one-fifth cut, first position guides. Place the guides in numeric order in your file drawer behind the card file. These two guides are the "file drawers" with which you will be working.

3. Affix labels 49–67 and 50–67 to any two previously used one-fifth cut, second position guides. Place the guides behind the 67 guide.

4. Affix labels 41–68 and 42–68 to any two previously used one-fifth cut, second position guides. Place the guides behind the 68 guide. You now have two partially complete drawers ready to receive folders filed by the terminal-digit method.

5. Affix twelve labels with 6-digit numbers to any previously used one-third cut, third position folders. Place the folders in a stack in front of you where they will be easily accessible as you work.

6. Remove from Forms Pad 4 twelve cards (numbered 17 to 28 in the lower right corners) that you will need for the alphabetic card file. Place these cards in alphabetic order with the cards used in Job 11. You will have a total of 28 cards, only 15 of which will be used in Job 12. Place the cards in front of you where they are easily accessible; you will remove cards as needed from the stack of 28.

7. Select the following pieces of correspondence, keeping them in numeric order: 1 through 15, a total of 15 records. Be sure to keep them in numeric order so that the numbers you will assign to them will be correct.

Filing Procedures

1. a. As you look at each record, find the alphabetic file card for that correspondent. Since your cards are in alphabetic order, you can quickly locate the needed card. When you have located the card, look at your Accession Log to determine the number to be assigned to that correspondent (or subject). With your colored pencil, write the correspondent name (or subject) in indexed order beside the number in the log. Then write the number in the upper right corner of the file card and the record. Remember also to code any cross-reference file card with the same number followed by an X. File the card or cards immediately in the card file.

   b. After you assign a number, locate the correspondingly numbered folder you have prepared and insert the record into the folder. Sort the folder by its terminal digit into a stack to be filed later. Since you will be working with only 15 records, code all of them and insert them into their folders before you file the folders. (If you had not already done so, you would have to inspect each record and code the filing segment as you did for the alphabetic filing method.)

   c. Code each record with the next available number in the Accession Log, using a colored pencil to distinguish these numbers from others that have previously been marked on the record. The number on the file card and the number on the record must always be the same for each correspondent.

   d. Specific instructions for the first five pieces follow:

   #1: From your stack of printed file cards, find the one for Donna Edwards. Check your Accession Log to determine that number 20 42 68 will be assigned to her. Write her name in indexed order in the Accession Log. With your colored pencil, legibly write *20 42 68* in the upper right corner of the card and record. Select the folder labeled 20 42 68 and place the record in it. File the card in your card file behind the E guide and sort the folder into a 68 stack to be filed later.

#2: Find the card for The Crystal Net, Inc., and refer to your Accession Log. Number 21 42 68 will be assigned to this correspondent. Write the name in indexed order on that line. Legibly write *21 42 68* on the card and on #2. Select folder 21 42 68 and insert #2 into it. File the card in the card file and sort the folder into the 68 stack for later filing.

#3: Reference to your Accession Log shows 22 42 68 will be assigned to Mr. Chas. S. Baker. Write his name in indexed order beside that number. Find his card and write that number on the card and on #3. Select the correspondingly labeled folder (22 42 68) and insert the record into it. File the card in the card file behind the B guide and sort the folder into the 68 stack.

#4: Find the original and cross-reference cards for Dr. Bekey and consult your Accession Log. Number 23 41 68 is the next number to be assigned. Write her name beside it in indexed order. Write that number on the cards and on #4. Select the correspondingly labeled folder and insert the record into it. File the original card in the B section and the cross-reference in the C section of the card file. Sort the folder into the 68 stack.

#5: This piece is an application letter, and Auric Systems, Inc. is likely to receive more correspondence about that subject. Write *Applications* beside 24 41 68 in the Accession Log. Write that number on the file cards for Applications and Chris Carter and on piece #5. File both cards in the card file and place #5 in the 24 41 68 folder. Sort the folder into the 68 stack.

2. Continue assigning numbers to the remaining records. Comments about some of the pieces follow:

#9: Find the original and cross-reference cards for Allen R. David. Write the name in the Accession Log and code the original card, the cross-reference card, and the letter. File both cards, place the letter in the 52 50 67 folder, and sort the folder into the 67 stack.

#10: Remember to code both the cross-reference card and the original card for ELITE, Inc.

#11: This record is the second one for Above & Beyond Insurance Co. Look up the assigned number in the card file. Code and file the letter in the proper folder in the 68 stack (most recently dated record in front).

#13: This record is the second one for The Crystal Net, Inc.

3. a. When you have completed piece #15, you are ready to file the numbered folders. Work with the 67 stack first. Sort the folders in the 67 stack by the secondary numbers. You should have three folders with 49 and three folders with 50. File the 49–67 folders behind the 49–67 guide according to the numeric sequence of their tertiary numbers.

File the 50–67 folders behind the 50–67 guide according to the numeric sequence of their tertiary numbers. When you have inserted the six folders into your file drawer, the order of the three guides and six folders will be as follows:

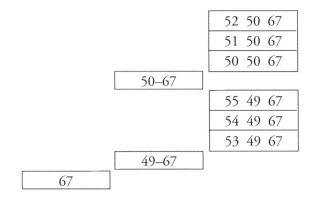

When glancing at the contents of the folders, you will see that alphabetic order is not maintained. Alphabetic order is found only in the card file, to which you must refer each time a record is to be stored or retrieved.

b.   Take the stack of 68 folders; separate them by the secondary digits (41 and 42) and file them behind the correct guide, 41–68 or 42–68, according to the tertiary numbers. When you have finished, you will have 12 folders in your file.

4.   On Report Sheet 12, indicate the appearance of your terminal-digit file by completing the captions on the folder tabs. You will find on the report sheet more folder tabs than you need. Indicate only the captions you have in your file and leave the remaining tabs blank.

5.   On a separate piece of paper, report the contents of your card file by listing in alphabetic order the full indexed name on each card and the code number assigned to each, as you did in Job 11.

6.   Submit Report Sheet 12 and your alphabetic card file list as your instructor directs. When your work has been checked, be sure to analyze any misfiles and understand any corrections made to your report sheet. Job 12 does not have a Finding Test.

Computer Activity

In this activity, you will enter codes for records in a numeric filing system and sort the records for terminal-digit filing.

1.   Create an *Access* file named *Job 12 Index*. Create a new table named **Records.** Create the fields shown in the following table. Make the ID field the primary key.

Field Name	Field Type
ID	Number
Name	Text
Folder	Number
Guide	Number
Drawer	Number

2. Select the following pieces of correspondence that you used in the manual part of this job: 1, 2, 3, 4, 5, 6, 7, 8, 9, 10, 12, and 14. Enter data for each piece in the database table:

    a.   Enter the correspondence piece number in the ID field.

    b.   Enter the correspondent's name in the Name field. For piece 5, enter **Applications, Chris Carter** in the Name field.

    c.   Referring to your manual file, enter the numbers assigned to that piece in the Folder, Guide, and Drawer fields.

3. Create a query named **Terminal-Digit Sort** based on the Records table. Include the Drawer, Guide, Folder, Name, and ID fields in the query results. Design the query to sort in ascending order by the Drawer field, then by the Guide field, and then by the Folder field. Run the query and print the query results table.

4. In which drawer is the record for Allen R. David stored?

5. How many records are stored in drawer 68?

6. In drawer 67, how many records are shown for guide 50?

Care of Supplies

When instructed to do so:

1. Remove the correspondence pieces from the folders, arrange them in original 1 through 45 numeric order, and place them in the Supplies 2 Envelope.

2. Remove the numeric guides and folders from your file drawer and place them in the Supplies 2 Envelope.

3. Remove the alphabetic file cards and arrange all the cards in 1 through 28 numeric order; place them in the Supplies 2 Envelope.

4. Remove the card file guides and place them in the Supplies 2 Envelope.

5. If labels for other jobs are on the same sheet as Job 12 labels, store the sheet of labels in the Supplies 1 Envelope for later use.

Job 13

Geographic Filing

The objective of this job is to construct and use a geographic file by the location name guide plan. You will file the cards from Jobs 1 and 2 into geographic order. The names of the persons and businesses on the cards are the names of cell phone customers. Auric Systems, Inc. has customers located in the state of Illinois. The Chicago, Illinois, central office maintains the database from customers in all areas of the state. In this job, you will arrange the cards in geographic order.

Supplies Needed

- File drawer
- 1 one-fifth cut, first position guide (any used previously)
- 8 one-fifth cut, second position guides (any used previously)
- Cards 1 through 27 (used previously in Jobs 1 and 2) (Supplies 2 Envelope)
- Sheet of self-adhesive labels, Job 13 (Supplies 1 Envelope)
- Report Sheet 13 (Data CD)
- Pencil

File Setup

1. Remove the sheet containing labels for Job 13. Affix the ILLINOIS label to a previously used one-fifth cut, first position guide. Place the guide at the front of the file drawer.

2. Affix the CHICAGO, EVANSTON, GLENCOE, NORTHBROOK, OAK LAWN, OAK PARK, PARK RIDGE, and WAUKEGAN labels to any eight previously used one-fifth cut, second position guides. Place each of these city guides in the file drawer behind the ILLINOIS guide, as shown below.

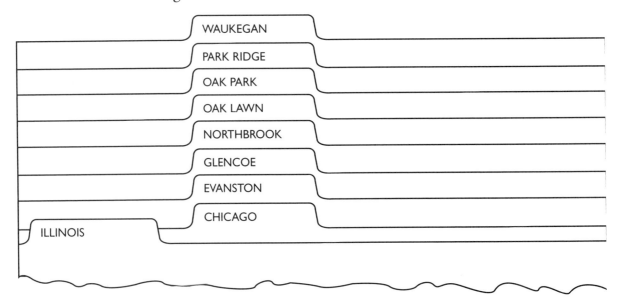

3. Remove cards 1 through 27 from the stack of 54 cards used in Jobs 1 and 2. Verify that they are in numeric order.

General Information

In an actual geographic filing system, an alphabetic card file of correspondents' names is necessary because records may be requested by name when the location of the correspondent has been forgotten or is not known. Cross-references needed for alternate correspondents' names are made for the alphabetic card file only. Cross-references to alternative locations are made for the geographic file only. For the purposes of this job, you will not set up an alphabetic card file or prepare cross-references. Remember that in an actual office, however, a geographic filing system would include an alphabetic card file and cross-references.

Filing Procedures

1. Code the location of each correspondent (whose name you have previously coded for another job) by circling the state and city names and numbering them in order of consideration. The state is considered first, then the city. The next units for filing purposes are in the name of the correspondent. An example for the state and city names is shown below:

2. Code the cards one at a time and rough sort them into stacks by city as you do so.

3. File the cards behind the proper city guides in your file drawer. For cards that bear the same city name, use the correspondent names to determine order according to the rules for alphabetic filing.

4. Report the order of the contents of your file drawer on Report Sheet 13. Beginning at the bottom of each column, list the numbers of the cards as they are filed in order behind each guide.

5. Check your report sheet as your instructor directs. Keep the contents of your file drawer intact. When your work has been checked, be sure that you understand any filing errors that were made. Job 13 does not have a Finding Test.

Computer Activity

In this activity, you will sort database records for geographic filing.

1. Locate the *Access* file *Job 13 Customers* in the data files. Copy the file to your working folder on a hard drive or removable storage device.

2. Open the Wireless table, which contains data for pieces 1 through 27 that you used in the manual portion of this job.

3. Insert a new text field named **Index Order** after the ID field. Enter the organization's name or the person's complete name in indexing order in the Index Order field. Include the title and suffix, if given, for personal names. Remember to omit the punctuation in this field. Using an Index Order field will allow you to sort the database records for individuals and organizations in the same field.

4. Create a query named **Geographic Sort** based on the Wireless table. Include the City, Index Order, and ID fields in the query results table. Sort the data by the City field and then by the Index Order field. Run the query and print the query results table.

5. In the Geographic Sort query results, how many records have "Chicago" in the City field?

6. Sort the Wireless table in ascending order by the Index Order field. What is the ID number of the first record?

7. What is the name of the person (in index order) who lives in Waukegan?

Care of Supplies

When instructed to do so:

1. Remove the cards from the file drawer, arrange them in 1 through 27 numeric order, and place them in the Supplies 2 Envelope.

2. Remove the guides and place them in the Supplies 2 Envelope.

3. Dismantle your file drawer and place it in the simulation envelope.